AMERICAN EDUCATION

Its Men,

Ideas,

and

Institutions

Advisory Editor

Lawrence A. Cremin
Frederick A. P. Barnard Professor of Education
Teachers College, Columbia University

AMERICAN EDUCATION: *Its Men, Ideas, and Institutions*
presents selected works of thought and scholarship that have
long been out of print or otherwise unavailable. Inevitably, such
works will include particular ideas and doctrines that have been
outmoded or superseded by more recent research. Nevertheless,
all retain their place in the literature, having influenced educational thought and practice in their own time and having provided
the basis for subsequent scholarship.

STUDIES IN
EARLY GRADUATE EDUCATION

THE JOHNS HOPKINS, CLARK UNIVERSITY, THE UNIVERSITY OF CHICAGO

By W. CARSON RYAN

ARNO PRESS & THE NEW YORK TIMES
*New York * 1971*

Reprint Edition 1971 by Arno Press Inc.

Reprinted from a copy in
  The Newark Public Library

American Education:
  Its Men, Ideas, and Institutions - Series II
  ISBN for complete set: 0-405-03600-0
  See last pages of this volume for titles

Manufactured in the United States of America

Library of Congress Cataloging in Publication Data

Ryan, Will Carson, 1885-
    Studies in early graduate education.
    (Carnegie Foundation for the Advancement of
Teaching. Bulletin no. 30) (American education:
its men, ideas, and institutions. Series II)
    Reprint of the 1939 ed.
    Bibliography: p.
    1. Johns Hopkins University--Graduate work.
2. Clark University, Worcester, Mass.--Graduate
work. 3. Chicago. University--Graduate work.
I. Title. II. Series. III. Series: American
education: its men, ideas, and institutions.
Series II.
LB2371.R9 1971   378.1'553'0973   73-165729
ISBN 0-405-03718-X

STUDIES IN
EARLY GRADUATE EDUCATION

THE JOHNS HOPKINS, CLARK UNIVERSITY,
THE UNIVERSITY OF CHICAGO

By W. CARSON RYAN

STAFF ASSOCIATE
CARNEGIE FOUNDATION FOR THE ADVANCEMENT OF TEACHING

WITH A PREFACE BY WALTER A. JESSUP

PRESIDENT OF THE FOUNDATION

BULLETIN NUMBER THIRTY

NEW YORK
THE CARNEGIE FOUNDATION
FOR THE ADVANCEMENT OF TEACHING
522 FIFTH AVENUE
1939

D. B. UPDIKE · THE MERRYMOUNT PRESS · BOSTON

CONTENTS

CONTENTS

PREFACE

INTEREST in graduate education is widespread. Upwards of eighty thousand students are enrolled in courses leading to advanced degrees. For the college or university, graduate education has become, as it were, "big business." The quality of learning at this level, the calibre of the men and women admitted to graduate schools, the relation of advanced teaching and research to other parts of the provision for college, university, technical, and professional training—all these matters involve questions that are today giving serious concern to the universities and to students of higher education generally.

The growth in graduate education is recent. There are men, active in academic circles, who have lived through the whole period of expansion. The part played by the Johns Hopkins University, Clark University, and the University of Chicago is generally recognized. Indeed, the patterns of present-day graduate work in this country derive largely from these first efforts. What, if anything, can we learn from the early experiences of these acknowledged American pioneers? Were their achievements such that they may throw light on the problems we face in the university on the graduate level today?

This bulletin has been prepared in the hope that it may be possible to find at least a partial answer to the question. Was the success at Hopkins, for example—instrumental, as President Eliot asserted, in enabling Harvard and other established institutions to develop their graduate programs—valid chiefly for the 'eighties or 'nineties? Or does it contain elements that are significant for American higher education of our time, especially in the graduate schools?

This is the day of huge numbers, in graduate training as in almost everything else. Hopkins and Clark were small institutions—very small as compared with universities today. Chicago, while much larger from the start than the other two, contrived to retain some of the intimacy and informality usually associated with smaller institutions—though not always found there. The handful of masters' and doctors' degrees have become thousands and even tens of thousands every year; the "seminars" of more or less hand-picked "fellows" are now often as large and impersonal as the largest lecture courses once were; universities are experimenting with modern instruments of scientific measurement and evaluation as a possible means of determining how best to proceed in dealing with the vast numbers who now more or less as a matter of course "go on to graduate work." It may be that the changes are so great and of such a character that the methods of these pioneer institutions do not apply. If, however, the experience of what seem to us like simpler days can in the slightest degree help us to find our way in the present situation we should take advantage of it. In any case, the stories of the graduate work in these three early universities are interesting and worthy of consideration. We may even find that some of our own complexities are unnecessary and that a measure of simplification is possible.

The method of the present study is largely descriptive. Mr. Ryan has made little or no attempt to pass judgment on the work of the three universities. Rather, he has attempted to describe the beginnings of the institutions, to analyze various elements in each situation, and to suggest some of the factors that appear to have been significant in bringing about the admitted successes that were achieved. The accounts of the three institutions have been written in such a way, it is hoped, that the reader will be encouraged to draw his own conclusions.

In preparing these descriptions the author used first-hand sources of information wherever possible: contemporary circulars and catalogue announcements; presidents' reports and addresses; official and unofficial correspondence and other unpublished materials; and interviews with surviving teachers, scholars, and research men who themselves participated in the work of the three institutions in the early days. Indispensable help in securing access to unpublished writings and other original data was provided by Mr. John C. French, librarian of the Johns Hopkins University Library, and by Miss Elisabeth Gilman, daughter of President Daniel C. Gilman, who made important papers of her father's available; by the library authorities at Clark University and by Dr. Robert G. Hall, of Portland, Oregon, who permitted detailed examination of manuscripts and other invaluable papers left by his father, Dr. G. Stanley Hall; by Professor

Samuel N. Harper, son of President William Rainey Harper, who read one of the first drafts of the section of the study dealing with Dr. Harper's career, and by the administrative officers and staff of the University of Chicago who furnished access to the Harper correspondence in the files of the President's office at the University.

Mr. Ryan personally interviewed many persons who had intimate and first-hand knowledge of these pioneering enterprises: Frederick E. Bolton, William L. Bryan, William H. Burnham, S. P. Capen, H. H. Donaldson, Abraham Flexner, Frank R. Lillie, E. L. Lindley, Warren P. Lombard, Henry D. Sheldon. Dr. Nicholas Murray Butler was especially helpful; he has had the role of professional observer from the very beginning. Interviews and correspondence with such men as these on the work of the institutions they knew give to parts of the description a sharpness of focus, it is believed, that would have hardly been possible in any other way.

The text of the volume was also submitted in proofs to present-day administrative officers and certain faculty members of the universities concerned in order to provide a further check on accuracy.

Funds for the inquiry and for publication of results have generously been made available by Carnegie Corporation of New York.

. . .

Study of graduate instruction in the United States was commenced for the Carnegie Foundation for the Advancement of Teaching by Henry Suzzallo in 1927 with the support of Carnegie Corporation of New York. After Dr. Suzzallo assumed the presidency of the Foundation he carried the study forward, and much material germane to it was gathered by him and by others. Mr. Ryan's inquiry deals with initial efforts in a field of American higher education one of whose finest products, most inspired scholars, and most inspiring teachers was Henry Suzzallo, president of the Carnegie Foundation from August 1, 1930, until his untimely death September 25, 1933.

WALTER A. JESSUP.

April, 1939

Permission to quote: Acknowledgment for permission to quote is made to the following: American Journal of Psychology; D. Appleton-Century Co.; Bobbs-Merrill Co.; Clark University Library; Columbia University Press; Dodd, Mead and Co.; Educational Record; Harvard University Press; Houghton Mifflin Co.; Johns Hopkins Alumni Magazine; Johns Hopkins University Press; Journal of Political Economy; Longmans, Green and Co.; The MacMillan Co.; National Academy of Sciences; New International Encyclopedia; Psychological Review; School and Society; School Review; Science; Charles Scribner's Sons; G. E. Stechert and Co.; University of Chicago Press; Viking Press.

STUDIES IN EARLY GRADUATE EDUCATION

INTRODUCTION

"WE have, as yet, no near approach to a real university in America,"
a committee of the National Teachers' Association reported at
the Trenton meeting of 1869. What the committee meant, as a
detailed reading of its able report will show, was that no higher institution
then existing in the United States was engaged in advanced teaching and
research beyond the limitations of the traditional college. "No competent
nation may stand acquitted before its own conscience and the enlightened
judgment of the world until it can point to one such center of original investigation and educational power," the committee declared.[1]

Within the next two decades following the publication of the National
Teachers' Association report, three institutions were established in different
parts of the country to do specifically what the committee had recommended
—provide advanced education, mainly or exclusively on the graduate level,
and "enlarge the boundaries of human knowledge by means of researches and
investigations." These three institutions were the Johns Hopkins University,
Baltimore, Maryland, which opened its doors in 1876; Clark University,
Worcester, Massachusetts, inaugurated in 1888; and the University of Chicago, which began its activities in 1890.

Of the importance of these three pioneering universities for subsequent
developments in American higher education, especially in the graduate
schools, there can be little doubt. The value of the Johns Hopkins contribution has been repeatedly acknowledged, but never more explicitly than
by President Charles William Eliot, of Harvard University, at the Hopkins
twenty-fifth anniversary. Addressing the head of Johns Hopkins on this
occasion Dr. Eliot said:

> President Gilman, your first achievement here, with the help of your col-
> leagues, your students, and your trustees, has been, to my thinking—and
> I have had good means of observation—the creation of a school of grad-
> uate studies which not only has been in itself a strong and potent school,
> but which has lifted every other university in the country in its depart-
> ments of arts and sciences. I want to testify that the graduate school of
> Harvard University, started feebly in 1870 and in 1871, did not thrive
> until the example of Johns Hopkins forced our faculty to put their strength
> into the development of our instruction for graduates. And what was true

---

[1] United States Commissioner of Education, *Annual Report* for 1870, p. 418. J. W. Hoyt, of Wisconsin,
was chairman of the committee, and he had as his colleagues such educational leaders of the period as
J. P. Wickersham, of Pennsylvania, and T. W. Bicknell, of Rhode Island.

of Harvard was true of every other university in the land which aspired to create an advanced school of arts and sciences.[2]

President Eliot's words on this occasion are all the more significant when taken in connection with the fact that in a conference with the Hopkins trustees in 1874 he had put himself on record as convinced that what was proposed in Baltimore could not succeed, on the ground that no institution, old or young, could cut loose from the educational foundations of the community in which it was placed. "We at Harvard," Mr. Eliot had said, "could not deliberately undertake to give only a high degree of education for a few. We could not deliberately undertake that, not even if we were starting anew."[3]

BEFORE JOHNS HOPKINS

Recognition of the need for a more advanced type of university education in America goes back to a period long before that of Charles William Eliot or the report of the National Teachers' Association committee of 1869. For several generations educational leaders had been voicing dissatisfaction with the American college in relation to the needs of the growing nation, and here and there individuals were trying to introduce changes. When, in 1849, President Francis Wayland, of Brown University, faced with declining enrollments at his institution, dramatically tendered his resignation, he stated that he took the action because he was convinced that the colleges of the day "were not meeting the educational wants of the country" and "our whole system of instruction needs an honest, thorough, and careful revision." Invited by the trustees of Brown to review the situation, he and his colleagues on the investigating committee presented a report that depicted the inadequacies of the American college and made specific recommendations for change.[4] The old institutions on colonial foundations had done well enough in their early period, he said, "but with the present century a new era dawned upon the world," an era in which science must be utilized to direct human labors, and one in which dependence upon a university program limited mainly to Greek, Latin, and the elements of mathematics was "plainly impossible." He cited the opinion of George Ticknor, who had

[2] Charles William Eliot, Address at the twenty-fifth anniversary of Johns Hopkins University, February 21, 1902.

[3] As quoted in Henry James, *Charles William Eliot*, Boston and New York, Houghton Mifflin Company, 1930, vol. II, p. 5.

[4] Report to the Corporation of Brown University on Changes in the System of Collegiate Education, Providence, George H. Whitney, 1850. See also: *A Memoir of the Life and Labors of Francis Wayland*, by Francis Wayland and H. L. Wayland, New York, Sheldon and Company, 1867, vol. II, pp. 83 ff.

pointed out that it was costing Americans more to be "very imperfectly educated" than it would to enjoy the great advantages of some of the best universities on the continent of Europe. President Wayland in his report attacked the American college for its coddling process with youth, as well as for its unsuccessful attempt to mix the old and the new learning. He recommended additional courses to meet the needs of various groups in the community, abandonment of the fixed four-year college course, and in its place a flexible arrangement whereby "every student might study what he chose, all that he chose, and nothing but what he chose."

At the time President Wayland was telling the Corporation at Brown what university needs were, a friend and college associate of his from the old Union College days, Henry Philip Tappan, soon to be the first president of the University of Michigan, was inquiring whether "there really is any good reason why we should not create in our country at least one great institution of learning that may vie with the best of the old world?" "Have we not," he asked, "the means in abundance? Shall the little principalities of Germany surpass these wealthy and powerful States?" In his book, published in 1851, Tappan pointed out that the advantages of the German universities to which so many Americans were repairing were mainly two: "First, they are purely universities, without any admixture of collegial tuition. Secondly, they are complete as universities, providing libraries and all other materials of learning, and having professors of eminence to lecture on theology, law, and medicine, the philosophical, mathematical, natural, philological, and political sciences, on history and geography, on the history and principles of art, in fine, upon every branch of human knowledge."[5]

Twenty years later the discussion had become more widespread and intense. Hundreds of Americans had by this time gone to the continent of Europe for advanced university work, and many of them were critical of conditions at home. The report of the Teachers Association quoted at the outset of this discussion is representative. When Noah Porter assumed his duties as president of Yale in 1871 he spoke of the "breeze of public interest and public criticism which is now blowing so freshly through the halls of ancient learning," and thought it was certain to bring life and vigor. He did express some fear that in the sweep of change the past might be neglected, but on the other hand he recognized that "every age has its own methods, its own forms of scientific inquiry," and higher institutions could not afford to estrange themselves from these in any "devotion to routine of academic

[5] Henry P. Tappan, *University Education*, New York, George P. Putnam, 1851, pp. 43–44. See also: Charles M. Perry, *Henry Philip Tappan*, Ann Arbor, University of Michigan Press, 1933.

instruction or the prosecution of learned researches." President James Burrill Angell in his inaugural address at the University of Michigan in 1871 referred to the discussion of college and university education that had been taking place as the result of the utterances of Wayland, Tappan, Eliot, and others, saying that it was more important than all such previous discussion since the planting of the New England colonies. Dr. Angell made a plea for at least "a few American universities, which shall be to our high schools and even to some of our colleges what the universities of Europe are to the secondary schools of England, the lycées of France, and the gymnasia of Germany." He urged educators not to be in too much of a hurry, not to spoil good colleges to make inferior universities, and to look beyond the externals. "I fear," he said, "that the public do not sufficiently understand that the essential thing in a university is *men*, both in the students' seats and in the professors' chairs."

Wherever such pupils and such teachers are pursuing the most generous culture of a civilized age, there are the essential constituents of a university, though as in Bologna in the 13th century the instruction is given in private houses of most modest structure, or though masters and disciples dwell in hovels of osier and thatch, like Abelhard and his followers on the wild banks of the Ardrissan. The youthful Plato hanging on the lips of the bare-footed Socrates in the streets of Athens—can we find in the world a picture of a more fruitful university culture than that?[6]

Daniel Coit Gilman in the later years of his life described conditions in respect to advanced university instruction during the 'fifties and 'sixties in terms of his own experience:

Opportunities for advanced, not professional, studies were then scanty in this country. In the older colleges certain graduate courses were attended by a small number of followers—but the teachers were for the most part absorbed with undergraduate instruction, and could give but little time to the few who sought their guidance. Probably my experience was not unusual. After taking the degree of Bachelor of Arts in Yale College, I was undecided what profession to follow. The effect of the collegiate discipline, which "introduced" me, according to the phrase of the day, to not less than twenty subjects in the senior year, was to arouse an interest of about equal intensity in as many branches of knowledge. I remained a year at New Haven as a resident graduate. President Woolsey, whom I consulted, asked me to read Rau's *Political Economy* and come and tell him its contents; I did not accept the challenge. I asked Professor Hadley

[6] Exercises at the Inauguration of President Angell. Ann Arbor, published by the University, 1871, pp. 9, 12.

if I might read Greek with him; he declined my proposal. Professor Porter did give me some guidance in reading, especially in German. I had many talks of an inspiring nature with Professor Dana—but, on the whole, I think that the year was wasted. The next autumn I went to Cambridge and called upon President Sparks, to learn what opportunities were there open. "You can hear Professor Agassiz lecture," he said, "if you want to; and I believe Mr. Longfellow is reading Dante with a class." I did not find at Cambridge any better opportunities than I had found at New Haven— but in both places I learned to admire the great teachers, and to wish that there were better arrangements for enabling a graduate student to ascertain what could be enjoyed and to profit by the opportunities.[7]

EARLY EFFORTS AT ADVANCED INSTRUCTION: HARVARD, YALE, MICHIGAN, COLUMBIA, OTHER UNIVERSITIES

Not only were leaders in higher education talking about the necessity for change, but, as Gilman implies in the passage just quoted, some attempts to provide more advanced work had been made.

Graduate Instruction at Harvard

As early as 1825 Professor Ticknor had contrived to get into the new College Laws of that period what Morison, the historian of Harvard, characterizes as "the first provision for alumni of other colleges to become 'resident graduates.' " The Harvard catalogue for 1826–27 lists the names of five such resident graduates, one of them being none other than "Ralph W. Emerson, A.B." Ticknor intended this provision, Morison says, to be an entering wedge for postgraduate instruction, "but no such instruction was provided and no degree was open to resident graduates unless they were Harvard A.B.'s." The number of resident graduates seems never to have exceeded fifteen, and was usually much less than this; but around the middle of the century Charles Eliot Norton, William Watson Goodwin, Simon Newcomb, James K. Hosmer, and Charles Sanders Peirce were among those who had taken advantage of this "opportunity to continue a scholarly life in academic surroundings."[8]

President Eliot himself, according to Morison, traced the beginnings of graduate work back to the University Lectures, first provided under President Hill in 1863. These were courses of lectures, chiefly on scientific topics,

[7] Daniel Coit Gilman, *The Launching of a University*, New York, Dodd, Mead and Company, 1906, pp. 8–9.

[8] Samuel Eliot Morison, editor, *The Development of Harvard University Since the Inauguration of President Eliot*, Cambridge, Harvard University Press, 1930, pp. 452 ff.

given by Harvard professors and others. In the opening year of President Eliot's administration two "University Courses of Instruction" were established for "graduates, teachers, and other competent persons," both men and women. One of them, a philosophy course, was conducted by a staff of lecturers that included Emerson, John Fiske, and C. S. Peirce; the other, on modern literature, boasted a staff that had Lowell, Child, Whitney, and William Dean Howells, among others. Thirteen people took the work— four Harvard graduates in philosophy and nine in other fields—but the courses were not repeated.

A graduate department was created at Harvard in 1872; the mastership in arts was reformed, and higher degrees were established, but apparently "graduate students chiefly took elective studies they had been unable to take in college."

Early Graduate Work at Yale

At Yale some advanced work for graduates is reported in the early 'forties. In 1841 Edward E. Salisbury, a graduate of Yale in the class of 1832, was appointed Professor of Arabic and Sanskrit—without salary. Provision was made for advanced students in chemistry and "natural history" at about the same period in Professor Benjamin Silliman's laboratory, and in 1848 two new professorships were set up in "agricultural chemistry" and "practical or applied chemistry."[9] Later Yale catalogues mention the year 1847 as the date of the beginning of formal graduate work, "when such courses were definitely arranged and the Department of Philosophy and the Arts constituted, with this object in view."[10] The degree of Doctor of Philosophy was first offered in 1860, and the catalogue for 1869–70 lists a number of graduate students, including 26 in the Sheffield Scientific School. Among the changes of which President Woolsey spoke approvingly at the time of his retirement in 1870 was "the recent enlargement of the course for graduates in philology and science, brought about by the professors themselves." Explicit recognition of the "university principle," according to F. B. Dexter, is found in the consolidation in 1872, under the Department of Philosophy and the Arts, of all courses, both graduate and undergraduate, not included in Theology, Medicine, and Law, and also in the increase from seven to seventeen in the number of fellowships available for "graduate scholars." This action had followed the report of 1871 on "needs of the University"

[9] Franklin Bowditch Dexter, *Sketch of the History of Yale University*, New York, Henry Holt, 1887, pp. 63–65.

[10] Catalogue of Yale University, 1886–87. New Haven, Tuttle, Morehouse, and Taylor, Printers.

made by ten members of the Yale faculty (one of them being Daniel Coit Gilman) in which it was recommended, among other things, that steps be taken "to convert the College into a true university." This would require particularly, the report said, strengthening and expanding the faculty, since at that time there was only one member who could devote himself full-time to graduate studies.

Tappan and the University of Michigan

Reference has already been made to Henry Philip Tappan and his ideas for reform in higher education on the European university pattern. Tappan went from New York City in 1852 to head the new University of Michigan, where he endeavored to put into effect, under very great difficulties, some of the policies he considered essential. He was as definite as Gilman was to be twenty years later in his insistence upon the difference between "a mere professional and technical education" and that "large and generous culture which brings out the whole man and commits him to the active life with the capacity of estimating from the highest points of view all the knowledges and agencies which enter into the well-being and progress of society." The most practical education, he said, was not that which leads men soonest and most directly to practice, "but that which fits them best for practice."

In his efforts to carry out his ideas at Michigan Tappan thought it was necessary to "liberate the students," to "remove them from tutelage," and to treat them as adults pursuing their own purposes.[11] The new State university was not to be "a preparatory school for boys"; students were to be encouraged to be responsible citizens, living in the community rather than in the artificial life of dormitories. It was Tappan's intention, says W. B. Shaw, to make Michigan "a real university in the accepted European view."

> It was not long before he let the world know the University's intention to "open courses of lectures for those who have graduated at this and other institutions." He thus foreshadowed the development of true graduate work; he introduced a curriculum in the sciences; he suggested the seminar method of instruction; and he sought to gather about him a faculty in which every chair was filled by a man of proved ability and scholarly training.[12]

By 1858 the "University Course" here referred to was established, and Andrew D. White and Francis Brünnow had been secured as members of a

[11] Perry, *Henry Philip Tappan*, p. 232.

[12] W. B. Shaw, *A Short History of the University of Michigan*, Ann Arbor, George Wahr, 1937, p. 40.

faculty equipped to carry on advanced work with graduate students. The University was already possessed of one of the largest astronomical observatories in the world, and Brünnow, who had been brought from Germany to serve as Professor of Astronomy and Director of the Observatory, was starting a career in research and teaching that undoubtedly had much to do with producing "the long line of distinguished astronomers who have studied at Michigan."

Of course, in all this there were difficulties. President Tappan was appreciated by some as a real educational pioneer; by others he was bitterly attacked and his plans were denounced as designed to "Prussianize" the good citizens of Michigan through their State university. Before Tappan finally lost out, however, he had spent eleven years at Ann Arbor and had helped build up a concept of higher education that went far beyond the confines of Michigan. "I found," said President James B. Angell in describing years later conditions at Michigan when he went there, "that the University had been inspired to a considerable extent by German ideals of education and was shaped under broader and more generous views of university life than most of the eastern colleges."[13] In 1902 Andrew D. White said of Tappan: "To him, more than to any other, is due the fact that, about the year 1850, out of the old system of sectarian instruction, mainly in petty colleges obedient to deteriorated traditions of English methods, there began to be developed *universities*—drawing their ideals and methods largely from Germany."[14]

It is worth noting that in 1881, when Henry Philip Tappan's death was announced from his residence abroad (he had never revisited Ann Arbor), the resolutions adopted by the Senate of the University of Michigan paid tribute to his foresight and leadership: "He saw better than others did, that . . . the chief need was not stately halls and aspiring chapels, but educated and able men."

Graduate Beginnings at Columbia

Various attempts were made at Columbia about the middle of the century and later to institute advanced university work. In 1852 a committee was appointed to report upon "the expediency of engrafting upon the foundation of this College a scheme of University professorships and lectures in the higher departments of letters and science," and the following year, when

[13] *The Reminiscences of James Burrill Angell*, New York, Longmans, Green, 1912, pp. 226–227.

[14] Quoted in Perry, *Henry Philip Tappan*, p. 248. See also: Andrew D. White, *Autobiography*, vol. I, pp. 276–281.

removal of the College to a new site was under discussion, another committee was instructed to look into the question "whether it would be expedient to establish a system of university education," supplementary to the undergraduate course or otherwise. The report was favorable but hesitant.[15] In 1854 resolutions respecting a graduate course of study were presented to the committee, and a recommendation was brought in for "supplemental courses in continuation of the studies of the first three years, solely for higher culture in learning and science." The plan as approved called for specialization in the senior year, to be followed by work in graduate schools—a School of Letters, a School of Science, and a School of Jurisprudence. A sharp distinction was thus drawn between the work of the first three years of the college course and that of the senior and graduate years. The three schools combined were to constitute the "University Course." Lectures under this plan were inaugurated in the fall of 1858, but except for the work in elementary law offered by Professor Theodore W. Dwight, and perhaps Professor Charles S. March's lectures on the English language, the program failed to receive the necessary support; "the Graduate School of Letters, Science, and Jurisprudence never really came into existence." The plan failed, Professor Munroe Smith states, "not because of intrinsic defects, but because it was put in operation at least two decades before the American public was ready for it."

President Barnard, however, did his best to keep the idea alive. In 1866, for example, he wrote: "Our own College . . . is the nucleus for what will one day be the great university of the city—possibly of the continent." Meanwhile, in 1864 the Columbia School of Mines, originally designed "to prepare well-educated mining engineers," began advanced work which soon covered five different scientific fields: mining engineering, civil engineering, metallurgy, analytic and applied chemistry, and geology and palaeontology. This was definitely understood to be part of a program which, the trustees said in 1864, contemplated "postgraduate instruction within the College." Graduate work developed under individual professors in the School of Mines, and the degree of Doctor of Philosophy at Columbia was first conferred in this school.[16]

One development in the 'seventies and early 'eighties at Columbia proved to be quite as important for university graduate work, especially in the

---

[15] Munroe Smith, *The University and the Non-professional Graduate Schools*, in History of Columbia University, 1754–1904, New York, Macmillan, 1904, pp. 199–304.

[16] Frederick P. Keppel, *Columbia*, New York, Oxford University Press, 1914, pp. 20–21. See also: J. H. Van Amringe, "The School of Mines," in *School of Mines Quarterly*, 10:339–51, January, 1890.

social sciences, as anything that took place at the Johns Hopkins University. In 1876 Professor John W. Burgess, already interested in graduate students from his experience at Amherst College, accepted a call to Columbia as professor of history, political science, and international law. Within four years Professor Burgess and his associates had brought about the establishment of a School of Political Science, on the example of the *Ecole Libres des Sciences Politiques* at Paris. The new plan provided a faculty composed of all professors already giving instruction in history, economics, public law, and political science to the senior class in the School of Arts and the classes of the School of Law, together with others of similar rank as they could be obtained. It set up a program of studies in history, economics, public law, and political philosophy, extending over a period of three years, with a degree of Ph.B. or A.B. to be conferred upon students completing the first year and of Ph.D. to be conferred upon students completing the curricula of the three years and presenting an approved thesis. Other elements in the plan conceived at the outset and ultimately realized were a system of graduate fellowships, a journal of the political sciences edited by the faculty (the *Political Science Quarterly*), an Academy of Political Science, and a series of treatises, textbooks, and monographs in the field of the social sciences.

As faculty and students or otherwise associated with it the School of Political Science had from its earliest days some of the most distinguished men ever engaged in this field: Munroe Smith, Frank J. Goodnow, Edwin R. A. Seligman, William A. Dunning, Herbert L. Osgood, William R. Shepherd, and Nicholas Murray Butler, who, though officially allied with philosophy, was one of those most actively concerned with the new venture.

From the beginning Professor Burgess had clearly in mind the relation of the School of Political Science to the whole university movement of the period. This is shown in an essay written in 1884 when the controversy over the new proposals was at its height, "The American University: When Shall It Be? Where Shall It Be? What Shall It Be?" In this essay Professor Burgess argued that "the entire realm of the Unknown belongs to the University; the primest function of the University is the discovery of *new* truth, the increase of knowledge in every direction." Years later, in his *Reminiscences*, Professor Burgess said that "the first principle of the system of education which the faculty of Political Science followed in all its work was free and untrammeled individual research and complete freedom of instruction in imparting the results of such research. . . . The progressive development of truth, instead of the monotonous maintenance of so-called established truth, was our principle."[17] It was natural that out of such an experience as the School of Political Science, graduates would go, as they did go in a steady stream, to fill posts in history, economics, sociology, constitutional, administrative, and international law, political science and philosophy, in leading universities everywhere; and that Columbia University's later expansion in graduate education should have come so largely from this pioneer work in political science.

At Other Institutions

Fabian Franklin in his biography of Gilman points out that "aspirations toward better university education existed in a number of places," and that efforts in the direction of more advanced university work were under way at various universities in the hands of exceptionally gifted or exceptionally equipped individuals. A few such instances have been indicated, and there undoubtedly were others. Brown University, for example, had some graduate work as early as 1859. At Princeton, V. L. Collins maintains, graduate students are recorded as early as 1760, and in President Witherspoon's time the College was rarely, if ever, without resident graduates—there were 23 in 1829. It was not until 1877, however, under President McCosh, that graduate courses were regularly authorized, when 42 men enrolled for them, 11 in pure science. In his farewell address of 1888 Dr. McCosh said that he had always encouraged postgraduate students, because it was from such students that the College hoped to produce scholars. "These graduate classes," he said, "will force us to become a university."[18] The "instructive success at the University of Virginia" was specifically cited by President Gilman as having received consideration in establishing the Johns Hopkins University. Gilman also emphasized the importance for university development of the Lawrence Scientific School of Harvard University and the Sheffield School of Science at New Haven as indicating that "the two oldest colleges of New England were ready to introduce instruction of an advanced character" in the various branches of natural and physical science, and especially Cornell University, since it "fortunately came under the guidance of one who was equally devoted to historical and scientific research."[19] The history of the University of Pennsylvania shows an understanding on the

[17] John W. Burgess, *Reminiscences of an American Scholar*, New York, Columbia University Press, 1934, p. 203. The essay of 1884 is reprinted in this volume, pp. 349–368.

[18] James McCosh, *Twenty Years of Princeton College*, New York, Scribner, 1888, p. 31.

[19] Daniel Coit Gilman, *The Launching of a University*, p. 3.

part of some of its leaders in the earliest days of the concept of a real university.

Hopkins, Clark, Chicago

It is against the background of these early discussions, abortive starts, and scattered pioneering efforts that the systematic work of the Johns Hopkins, Clark, and the University of Chicago can best be understood.

There is much more of continuity in the development of higher education in America than is sometimes assumed. The three institutions singled out for consideration in the present study were pioneers in a real sense, but they did not exist alone. They were directly related to the earlier period of controversy, exploration, and experimentation. Moreover, they were very closely related to each other. Dr. G. Stanley Hall left Baltimore and his laboratory of experimental psychology because he thought he saw an opportunity at Clark University to do advanced university work of a type thoroughly in accord with Daniel Coit Gilman's original purposes at the Hopkins. And three years after Clark University had started, President William Rainey Harper of the new University of Chicago, hard pressed for scientists to fill important positions in his institution, came to Worcester and invited from Clark University a number of its best men—men who had been "ideally prepared," as Dr. Hall afterward said, for graduate teaching and research. Like Hall, Harper took his point of departure in university innovation from the Johns Hopkins experiment. He believed the opportunity was at hand to do university work of high qualty, with the emphasis upon graduate research, on a scale never attained at Baltimore.

I
THE JOHNS HOPKINS: UNIVERSITY PIONEER

So quick she bloomed, she seemed to bloom at birth,
As Eve from Adam, or as he from earth.
Superb o'er slow increase of day on day,
Complete as Pallas she began her way;
Yet not from Jove's unwrinkled forehead sprung,
But long-time dreamed, and out of trouble wrung,
Fore-seen, wise-plann'd, pure child of thought and pain,
Leapt our Minerva from a mortal brain.

SIDNEY LANIER, *Ode to the Johns Hopkins University,* 1880

T HE founder of the Johns Hopkins University was not merely a wealthy man "whose benefactions by a happy chance turned out to be a notable and far-reaching contribution to human welfare." He was, says Dr. John C. French, head of the Hopkins library, "a significant figure in time and place, a man of much good sense and insight, in whose character there were some of the elements of greatness."[1]

A QUAKER MERCHANT

Born in Anne Arundel County, Maryland, in 1795, of Quaker family, Johns Hopkins at an early age became a successful merchant-trader, whose name was a household word far down the Valley of Virginia, and whose Conestoga wagons, "each crammed with merchandise sufficient to fill a small warehouse, with their spanking teams and jingling bells, were crossing and recrossing the Alleghenies, to the new states beyond."[2]

Freeing of the slaves on his plantation, to accord with Quaker "testimony" on slavery, is said to have made Johns Hopkins's father comparatively poor and cut short the boy's formal schooling at twelve years of age. As a lad of seventeen Johns Hopkins went to Baltimore to live and work with his uncle, Gerard Hopkins, who was a wholesale grocer and commission merchant. Two years later Gerard was designated by Baltimore Yearly Meeting to go to Ohio to attend the opening of the first Yearly Meeting of Friends in that State, and the nineteen-year-old nephew was left behind in charge of the business. Five years later Johns Hopkins was himself independently in trade, through the help of his uncle, and began amassing a fortune which ulti-

[1] John C. French, "Johns Hopkins, Founder," *The Johns Hopkins Alumni Magazine,* March, 1937, pp. 227–234.

[2] Allen Kerr Bond, *When the Hopkins Came to Baltimore,* Baltimore, Pegasus Press, 1927, p. 23.

mately reached eight million dollars and made him the leading capitalist of the city. Mr. Hopkins, early becoming interested in railroads, invested heavily in Baltimore and Ohio securities and served as chairman of the financial committee of the company from 1855 until his death in 1873. He is credited with having thrown the weight of his private fortune behind the railroad in the panics of 1857 and 1873, and "thus assured its solvency."[3] He built huge warehouses in Baltimore, and increased his fortune by banking and investment.

At precisely what period in his life and under what circumstances Johns Hopkins conceived the idea of devoting most of his fortune to a university and hospital is not known. He had never married, he and his cousin Elizabeth having yielded to the strong conviction of their family and associates against the marrying of cousins. The Maryland Academy of Sciences, Dr. Allen Bond says, cherishes a tradition that it was at a lunch in its old building on Mulberry Street that Mr. Hopkins finally decided upon the use of his wealth for the great endowment. Already, it appears from Dr. Bond's notes, he had been a donor to local charitable undertakings, especially the hospital, and had discussed the medical needs of Baltimore with various people. As for the university, Dr. French suggests that Mr. Hopkins doubtless recalled his own interrupted schooling and desired to provide young men of a later generation with the opportunity he had missed.[4] It is known, too, that he had learned from George Peabody, another Baltimore philanthropist, something of the satisfaction to be derived from educational benefactions.[5] In any case, Mr. Hopkins proceeded in 1867 to incorporate both a hospital and a university, bestowing $3,500,000 upon each, and naming for the two enterprises trustees "chosen with great care and singular skill."

THE HOPKINS TRUSTEES

All observers agree that the board of trustees for the proposed new university formed an unusual group of men. They represented, as Reverdy Johnson, Jr., their secretary, informed Dr. Gilman in a letter written in

---

[3] Dr. French, on whose account this statement is largely based, says: "It is entirely possible that the financial difficulties of the Baltimore and Ohio in the late eighties—difficulties which seriously affected the University—would have been averted if it had not been deprived by his death of his skillful guidance and support." (John C. French, "Johns Hopkins, Founder," p. 231.)

[4] Writing in 1905 Daniel Coit Gilman repeated a story he said was current to the effect that "a sagacious friend" had said to Mr. Hopkins: "There are two things which are sure to live—a university, for there will always be the youth to train; and a hospital, for there will always be the suffering to relieve." ("This germ, implanted in a large brain, soon bore fruit.")

[5] Daniel Coit Gilman, *The Launching of a University*, pp. 11–12.

1874, "the worth and intelligence of our city." The president of the board was Galloway Cheston, chairman of the finance committee of the Baltimore and Ohio Railroad—a "merchant and lover of flowers." Other members included John W. Garrett, president of the Baltimore and Ohio; George W. Dobbin and George William Brown, supreme court justices; Reverdy Johnson, Jr., with his law degree from Heidelberg and keen interest in French and German scholarship; and Dr. James Carey Thomas, a physician, father of Miss M. Carey Thomas who was later to be president of Bryn Mawr. In its religious affiliation the board was about evenly divided between Friends (Quakers), and other Protestant groups, chiefly Episcopalian.

The trustees held a meeting in June, 1870, six years before the actual opening of the University and three years before Mr. Hopkins's death. They seem to have been indefatigable. At a time when travel was much less customary than today they would get aboard a train and go round the country interviewing university presidents and others about the kind of university they should have and the type of man who might head it. They consulted, among others, Charles W. Eliot of Harvard, James B. Angell of Michigan, and Andrew D. White of Cornell, and they visited in a body Cambridge, New Haven, Ithaca, Ann Arbor, Philadelphia, Charlottesville, and other seats of learning.

Johns Hopkins gave his trustees a remarkably free hand. They were not to use the capital for buildings, and they were requested to keep intact the Baltimore and Ohio Railroad common stock that formed so large a part of the original holdings, but in other respects they were unrestricted. With a reputation for careful figuring in business deals Mr. Hopkins seems to have taken a broad view of the needs in this case. "As he walked the paths of Clifton in his last years and planned the inheritance he would leave behind him," says a recent writer, "the merchant forgot scruple and reservation, and threw all that he had on the side of human good."[6] The founder made no effort to unfold a plan, President Gilman stated. "He simply used one word—university—and he left it to his successors to declare its meaning in the light of the past, in the hope of the future." Moreover—

There is no indication that he was interested in one branch of knowledge more than another. He had no educational "fad." There is no evidence that he had read the writings of Cardinal Newman or of Mark Pattison, and none that the great parliamentary reports had come under his eye. He was a large-minded man who knew that the success of the foundation

[6] Broadus Mitchell in the *Johns Hopkins Alumni Magazine*, November, 1938, p. 3.

would depend upon the wisdom of those to whom its development was entrusted.[7]

The trustees, in turn, were willing to give opportunity and responsibility for direction to an educational leader as president. They were, to quote again one of their own number, a body of gentlemen who, "while at all times asserting independent thought and action, would not be disposed to throw obstacles or captious objections in the way of the presiding officer."[8]

Significant of the seriousness with which the trustees undertook their duties is the fact that the first books for the University library, purchased two years before the opening of the University, were secured in order that they might inform themselves about education in the United States and abroad. These books, as recorded in an old accessions list, were:

Higher Schools and Universities in Germany, by Matthew Arnold.
Sex in Education, by E. H. Clarke.
On the Cam, by W. Everett.
Classical Study, by S. H. Taylor.
Liberal Education of Women, by J. Orton.
College Words and Customs, by B. H. Hall.
Art Education, by Walter Smith.
Four Years at Yale.
Lectures and Reports on Education, by Horace Mann.
National Education, by J. H. Rigg.
American Colleges and the American Public, by Noah Porter.
History of Harvard University, by Josiah Quincy.
Five Years in an English University, by C. A. Bristed.
Culture Demanded by Modern Life, by E. L. Youmans.
Education Abroad, by B. G. Northrop.
The Conflict of Studies, by I. Todhunter.
Education, by Herbert Spencer.
The School and the Army in Germany and France, by General W. B. Hazen.
Vocal and Physical Training, by L. B. Monroe.
Pedagogics as a System, by Dr. J. K. Rosenkranz (translated by Anna C. Brackett).
Princeton College During the Eighteenth Century, by S. D. Alexander.
History of Williams College, by C. Durfee.

High quality for the new enterprise was apparently deep in the consciences of the trustees. "Often in private conversations and in official interviews," President Gilman said later, "I was charged to hold up the highest standard, to think of nothing but the best which was possible under the limitations

[7] Daniel Coit Gilman, *The Launching of a University*, p. 128.

[8] Reverdy Johnson, Jr., in Fabian Franklin's *Life of Daniel Coit Gilman*, New York, Dodd, Mead and Company, 1910, p. 184.

of a new establishment, in a country where the idea of the university had not been generally understood."[9]

A "University," not a "College"

For the most part the trustees understood that they were not to establish in Baltimore a typical "college," but something different—a "university."[10] It was not to be a local high school, nor a school of technology, nor a group of professional schools. It was to supplement and not to supplant existing institutions.

"Colleges" Baltimore already had. "The city," said President Gilman in his inaugural address, "maintains two excellent high schools for young ladies, and for young men a city college, so well organized, so well taught, and so well supported that it relieves our foundation of doing much which is called *collegiate* in distinction from *university* work." The trustees and the president of the new university were determined to seek students "mature enough to be profited by university education," at first from Baltimore and the South, but eventually on a national basis, "whenever the university's work and prestige should justify it." University instruction meant "liberal advanced instruction for those who want it; distinctive honors for those who need them; a special course for those who take no other; a combination of lectures, recitations, laboratory practices, field work and private instruction; the largest discretion allowed to the faculty consistent with the purposes in view."

As a university Johns Hopkins was not to be restricted to the conventional college years. "I see no advantage in our attempting to maintain the traditional four-year class system of the American college. . . . It is a collegiate rather than a university method. . . . I would have our university seek the good of individuals rather than of classes."[11] Later President Gilman was to look back upon the first twenty years and say:

> When the Johns Hopkins University was opened, many people, far and near, regretted that another college was founded. They saw no reason for it. Baltimore had its City College. The State of Maryland had St. John's. North and South were institutions which for years had been favorite places for the education of Maryland youth. No demand had been shown

[9] Johns Hopkins University, *Eleventh Annual Report of the President*, 1886, p. 6.

[10] Having selected a president, they "accepted his suggestion" on this point, according to Gilman (*The Launching of a University*, p. 7).

[11] Addresses at the Inauguration of Daniel C. Gilman as president of the Johns Hopkins University, Baltimore, 1876, p. 55.

by the people for any departure from the ancient land-marks. All was quiet. There were, however, a few persons who believed that it was possible to establish a new institution upon a new plan. They saw (or thought that they saw) the educational requirements of this country; and they desired to supply those wants without entering into any competition with other foundations. It was their purpose to enlarge the resources of American scholarship. They believed that the funds at command, if rightly employed, might give a strong impetus to learning and culture,—first in Baltimore, then in Maryland and the other Southern States, and, at length, throughout the entire land. Such aspirations were not quickly understood. They were received in certain quarters with incredulity; elsewhere with chilling curiosity; and occasionally with open hostility or avowed indifference. But those who were in charge had the courage of their convictions. They knew what strong desires were already manifested, in every part of the country, by young men of talents and ambition, for the opportunities of "university" education as distinct from "college" discipline; and, adding to this knowledge faith, the management announced its modest programme, very simple and unostentatious, and as modern as it was modest, but including (as was then believed) the germ of life and strength.[12]

President Gilman

On the advice of Eliot, Angell, and White, the trustees picked for the presidency Daniel Coit Gilman, then head of the University of California. President Gilman was appointed in December, 1874; he went to travel in Europe during 1875 in the interests of the new project, and the University opened in 1876.

A graduate of Yale in the class of 1852, Gilman had had an unusually varied educational experience. He had traveled abroad as a young man, serving in a more or less unofficial diplomatic capacity, visiting educational institutions in England and on the continent, especially in Germany, and writing down careful notes on the newer developments in university and technical training. Returning to New Haven in 1855, he was appointed assistant librarian of the Yale College library in 1856 and librarian two years later, and became professor of physical geography in 1863. For three years, 1856 to 1859, he served on a part-time basis as "acting school visitor" in the public schools of New Haven. In 1865 he took the newly created post of Secretary of the Connecticut State Board of Education, holding this for a year and then becoming secretary of the Sheffield Scientific School. He left New Haven in 1872 for his three years at the University of California.

12 Johns Hopkins University, *Twentieth Annual Report of the President*, 1896–97.

Gilman had long planned fundamental university changes, but the atmosphere of eastern universities of that day was not sympathetic to change. He had not been happy in the years at the University of California, mainly because of pressure brought by a legislature insistent upon a type of education that was at variance with Gilman's conception of what university education should be, and he welcomed the Baltimore invitation.

The new president was fully aware of the unusual variety of experience he had had in preparation for his work. He later summed up as follows his impressions of the three institutions of higher education with which he had been associated:

> Yale was a colonial foundation, wedded to precedents, where an effort was made to introduce new studies and new methods. California was a state institution, benefited by the so-called agricultural grant, where it was necessary to emphasize the importance of the liberal arts, in a community where the practical arts were sure to take care of themselves. Baltimore afforded an opportunity to develop a private endowment free from ecclesiastical or political control, where from the beginning the old and the new, the humanities and the sciences, theory and practice, could be generously promoted.

FACULTY AND STUDENTS

Prohibited by the terms of its grant from plunging immediately into an elaborate building program, the new university gave special attention to the human material essential for the type of enterprise that was planned.[13] Just as the trustees considered it their first duty to secure a head who was to be an educational leader, so the president's immediate and pressing task was to secure a faculty. Teaching staff and students were put ahead of everything else—not only ahead of educational buildings, but of "dormitories, commons, discipline, and degrees." Those in charge of the new university were determined to try to bring to Baltimore, as teachers and as students, the ablest minds they could attract—"we were to await the choice of a faculty before we matured any schemes of examination, instruction, and graduation.[14]

It was a very small faculty, as modern universities go, but it included,

---

[13] It is not meant to imply that physical plant was wholly disregarded. Professor Kemp Malone has shown that a considerable amount was spent for buildings during the first decade, mainly out of income, and that construction went forward even after the suspension of Baltimore and Ohio dividends. He warns against too easy an acceptance of the notion that "the university in 'the good old days' put its money into men, *not* into buildings." (*Johns Hopkins Alumni Magazine*, June, 1931, p. 307). The essential emphasis placed on persons, rather than physical plant, seems clear enough from the evidence, however.

[14] Daniel Coit Gilman, *The Launching of a University*, p. 12.

for mathematics, Professor J. J. Sylvester, of Cambridge, Woolwich, and London, "one of the foremost of European mathematicians"; as the leader of classical studies, Professor Basil L. Gildersleeve, from the University of Virginia; as director of the chemical laboratory and of instruction in chemistry, Professor Ira Remsen, from Williams College; to organize the work in biology ("a department then scarcely known in American institutions, but here regarded as of great importance with reference to the future school of medicine"), Professor H. Newell Martin, from Cambridge, England, a pupil of Professor Michael Foster and of Professor Huxley; as head of the department of physics, Professor Henry A. Rowland, who was then holding a subordinate position in the Rensselaer Polytechnic Institute, but whose contributions to scientific journals had attracted notice; and, as "collegiate professor," or "guide" to the undergraduate students, Professor Charles D. Morris, of New York, formerly a Fellow of Oriel College, Oxford. Three of the seven heads of departments were under thirty years of age.

In the selection of a staff of teachers for the university, President Gilman explained, the trustees had endeavored to consider especially "the devotion of the candidate to some particular line of study and the certainty of his eminence in that specialty"; the power to pursue independent and original investigation, and to inspire the young with enthusiasm for study and research; willingness to cooperate in building up a new institution, and freedom from tendencies toward ecclesiastical or sectional controversies. The trustees announced that they would not be governed by denominational or geographical consideration in the appointment of any teacher, but would endeavor to select the best person whose services they could secure, "irrespective of the place where he was trained, or the religious body with which he might be enrolled." Regard was also given to "those personal characteristics which cannot be overlooked . . . if the social relationship of a teacher to his colleagues, his pupils and their friends are to be harmoniously maintained."[15]

It had not been easy to select a faculty. Indeed, Gilman years later referred to this as "the first real difficulty." While the problem in this respect was perhaps not so serious as Harper found it at the University of Chicago, Gilman anticipated that it would be something of a task to secure the best men who were free to accept positions in a "new, uncertain, and, it must be acknowledged, somewhat risky organization." In writing about it afterward he declined to "recall the overtures made to men of mark, nor the overtures received from men of no mark." "Nor can I say," he added, "whether it was

[15] Bernard Christian Steiner, *The History of University Education in Maryland*, Baltimore, Johns Hopkins University Press, 1891, p. 61.

harder to eliminate from the list of candidates the second best, or to secure the best. All this it is well to forget. When I die, the memory of these anxieties and perplexities will forever disappear."[16]

But Dr. Gilman did leave on record the clear notion that, notwithstanding differences in training and experience, the original faculty "were full of enthusiasm, and we got on together without a discordant note."

We brought to the council room many prejudices and preferences derived from our previous training and from our personal idiosyncrasies. Two of the staff had been professors in the University of Virginia, two had been Fellows in the great English universities, two had received degrees in German universities and others had studied abroad, two had been connected with New England colleges, two had been teachers in scientific schools, and one had been at the head of a state university. Our discussions were free and familiar, as of friends around a council board. It was rarely, if ever, necessary to "make a motion" or to put a question to the vote. By processes well known to Friends, "the sense of the meeting" was taken and recorded.

It was our dominant purpose to hold on to the principles and adhere to the methods which experience had established in this and other countries, and at the same time to keep free from the slavery of traditions and conditions which are often more embarrassing and retarding than positive laws. We often reminded one another that the rule of today was liable to become the custom of tomorrow, the immemorial usage of next month, the iron-clad law of the future, and we tried to preserve spontaneity of action, not only for ourselves, but for our successors. . . .

Every head of a department was allowed the utmost freedom in its development, subject only to such control as was necessary for harmonious cooperation. He could select his own assistants, choose his own books and apparatus, devise his own plans of study,—always provided that he worked in concord with his fellows.[17]

The small staff of professors was supplemented by a systematic plan of lectures by distinguished visitors from other institutions—a feature of the program which had important results and will be discussed in more detail later.

As to students for the new university, it was the policy from the start "to care less for numbers than for merit; to maintain high standards of matriculation and graduation, to allow a wide latitude in respect to the choice of courses of instruction, and to give special facilities (such as fellow-

[16] Daniel Coit Gilman, *The Launching of a University*, p. 14.
[17] Ibid., p. 49.

ships and scholarships) to those who show unusual ability in any department of study."[18] One of the provisions of the Hopkins will called for the establishment of "such number of free scholarships in the said university as may be judicious" and to distribute these in terms of "character and intellectual promise." When the university opened, forty young men were enrolled as associate fellows and resident graduates. These had been graduated from American colleges in the ten years preceding; twelve had taken prolonged courses in Europe, six had the M.D., and six the Ph.D. "The Johns Hopkins University is said to be the only university in this country which has begun with such a staff of graduates," a contemporary newspaper account asserted.

OPENING OF THE UNIVERSITY

Dr. Gilman was inducted into office on February 22, 1876, with an address by President Eliot of Harvard. The University opened its doors to students in the fall, the formal opening being made memorable by an address by Professor Thomas Huxley, then on a lecture tour in the United States.

In his address at Gilman's inauguration, President Eliot emphasized the necessity for high standards of training. "Universities, wisely directed," he said, "store up the intellectual capital of the race, and become fountains of spiritual and moral power." Those in charge of the new enterprise were congratulated for founding in Baltimore "a worthy seat of learning and piety":

Here may young feet, shunning the sordid paths of low desire and worldly ambition, walk humbly in the steps of the illustrious dead—the poets, artists, philosophers, and statesmen of the past; here may fresh minds explore new fields and increase the sum of knowledge; here, from time to time, may great men be trained up to be leaders of the people; here may the irradiating light of genius sometimes flash out to rejoice mankind; above all, here may many generations of manly youth learn righteousness.

In the inaugural address President Gilman visualized the "unwonted activity" in higher education all over the world, described the hopes for the new university, making especially clear his distinction between "university" and "college," and closed by saying: "My life thus far has been spent in two universities, one full of honors, the other full of hopes; one led by experience, the other by expectations. May the lessons of both, the old and the new, be wisely blended here."

The choice of Professor Huxley as the opening lecturer was largely due to

---

[18] *Johns Hopkins University Register, 1880–81*, p. 21.

his eminence in biological studies and their interpretation. His appearance was the signal for a storm; Fabian Franklin has told how offended some religious people were that Huxley was chosen to give the lecture and that the program was not preceded by prayer.[19] Professor Huxley in his address paid tribute to the high ideals set up by those who were starting the University. He urged upon them breadth of educational provision, with abundant opportunities in history, physical sciences, and the creative arts. He stressed the significance of a hitherto neglected function of the university, namely, "to increase the stock of knowledge by the investigation of truth." It was ideas that were important, he said:

> The future of this world lies in the hands of those men who will supply the world with ideas and in some way furnish the masses of mankind who have not the time or the inclination or the capacity to think out things themselves with some theory of things that is not too absolutely inconsistent or too absolutely absurd to serve some practical purpose.

He called it the highest duty of a university to find a system that should discuss and protect the powers of artistic creation and the investigation of new truths that formed "the two great sides of active, or what we may call the original or creative, or investigative human mind." He saw real possibilities for the United States as a democracy, with dependence upon "intellectual clearness" and "moral worth" of the individual citizen.[20]

Few educational enterprises have had the almost instantaneous success of the Johns Hopkins University. Sidney Lanier's "So quick she bloomed, she seemed to bloom at birth," is not merely the expression of a poet's fancy; it described accurately what happened. There had been discussion of long years of development; and President Gilman had spoken in his inaugural address of the slow process that would be necessary. Actually, however, the University was a success from the outset; whatever local disappointments there may have been over the failure to erect a huge plant at Clifton, so far as the academic world was concerned the Johns Hopkins University was an accepted fact almost the instant it opened its doors, and within an incredibly few years it gave all the appearance of ripe maturity.

SIGNIFICANT ELEMENTS IN THE HOPKINS ACHIEVEMENT

Some of the elements that entered into the Johns Hopkins success have

---

[19] "Huxley was bad enough; Huxley without a prayer was intolerable." (*Life of Daniel Coit Gilman*, p. 221.)

[20] New York (weekly) *Tribune*, Extra No. 36, "Professor Huxley in America," pp. 7–14. Also in Huxley's *American Addresses*, D. Appleton and Company, 1877, pp. 100–127.

already been intimated—the wisdom of the donor and the trustees in setting up the original plan; the substantial nature of the financial resources; the definite effort to adjust to clearly recognized needs rather than to carry on a traditional educational enterprise; emphasis from the outset upon human qualities rather than physical plant and the mechanics of organization.

President Gilman's Leadership

With due allowance for the significance of these elements in the Johns Hopkins achievement, unquestionably the selection of Daniel Coit Gilman as president of the new university was a most important factor. "We have developed in this country," says Mr. Abraham Flexner, "a relatively small body of educational administrators who know the difference between significance and insignificance, and I should myself be inclined to place at the head of them Mr. Daniel Coit Gilman, who conceived the Johns Hopkins University."[21] The first great merit of President Gilman, wrote Fabian Franklin in 1910, was that "from the moment he was called to Baltimore, the object which he set before himself was that of making the institution which was to arise there under his guidance a means of supplying to the nation intellectual training of a higher order than could be obtained at existing colleges and universities." To take such a stand was one thing; to be able to carry his plans forward under the prevailing conditions was something different and much more difficult. As Dr. Franklin says:

> To be firm against local prejudices and desires when in conflict with the great end in view; to be uninfluenced by personal claims and unafraid of temporary complainings; to disappoint the natural hopes of those who were anxious to see imposing buildings and big crowds of students, and to await the recognition which attends the genuine achievement of a vital but not superficially showy result—these are things that look easy in the retrospect, but that did not seem by any means matters of course before the event.

Brief mention has already been made of Gilman's unusual preparation for such a piece of educational leadership as he undertook at Baltimore. His biographer, following him through the years in New Haven, finds that "all the forces of his nature, all the talents with which he was so plentifully endowed, were leading him and compelling him into the line of work in which he was to become preeminent as a leader."[22] At New Haven he had engaged

[21] *School and Society*, June 26, 1937, p. 871.
[22] Fabian Franklin, *Life of Daniel Coit Gilman*, p. 39.

in a variety of activities—in teaching; in raising funds; in administrative work in the college library and in the Scientific School ("then at the point of changing from two or three unconnected departments into an organized whole"); in writing for magazines and newspapers; in lecturing on education, especially science education. His part-time services as "acting school visitor" under the New Haven Board of Education had led to the establishment of a public high school in New Haven and the appointment of the first full-time superintendent of public schools for the city. He was especially interested in what was currently called "the new education," by which was meant an education that gave more nearly adequate attention to the natural sciences. Franklin makes the point that Gilman, having himself had a standard "classical" education, was an excellent advocate of science—he had studied various institutions in Europe where "the new education" had long been successfully established; he had a strong faith in the possibilities of human beings, and he understood clearly the principle of adaptation as opposed to imitation of successful educational enterprises elsewhere. As early as 1856 Gilman had prepared a "Proposed Plan for the Complete Organization of the School of Science Connected with Yale College," which included an appendix on the schools of science in Europe, and had published other articles on the place of education in science. He had been instrumental in securing for the Sheffield Scientific School the Federal aid that became available under the Morrill Act of 1862 for agricultural and technical instruction, and his own professorship of physical geography was made possible by the developments under the Morrill Act. He had taught for nine years, giving courses not only in physical geography, but also in political geography, history, and economics. Continuing as head of the library until 1865, he had then accepted appointment to the newly created position of secretary of the Connecticut State Board of Education, a post which he held for a year. In the first annual report of the board to the Legislature, Dr. Gilman had discussed the need for a sufficient supply of good teachers for the public schools of the State; reorganization of the State normal school; need for additional high schools; the evils of child labor in factories; the desirability of building up fewer but stronger schools to replace the poorly supported, small district schools; and the value of cooperation between the universities and colleges of the State and the public schools as "the only method by which a really strong and vigorous educational system could be built up."

Then, to cap it all, Dr. Gilman had been for three years the head of a newly established State university, an outgrowth of the Morrill Act—the University of California.

However one may estimate Dr. Gilman's abilities, the extraordinarily rich experiences through which he had passed must have given him an unusual preparation for the task of creating a new university. It was no accident that each of the educators consulted by the trustees named the same man as his candidate for president without knowing whom his colleague had recommended.[23]

A CLEARLY DEFINED PURPOSE

Rarely has an educational enterprise been launched with as clear a realization of important work to be done. "What are we aiming at?" President Gilman asked in one of the main sections of his inaugural address, and answered his own question succinctly:

An enduring foundation; a slow development; first local, then regional, then national influence; the most liberal promotion of all useful knowledge; the special provision of such departments as are elsewhere neglected in the country; a generous affiliation with all other institutions, avoiding interferences and engaging in no rivalry; the encouragement of research; the promotion of young men; and the advancement of individual scholars, who by their excellence will advance the sciences they pursue, and the society where they dwell.

The president and his trustees were resolved to accept that which they considered already determined, to avoid that which was obsolescent, to study that which was doubtful—"slowly making haste." President Nicholas Murray Butler and other observers have commented that in this respect the Johns Hopkins group were freer than any others of the same period in educational reform. Dr. Gilman believed that certain things were definitely settled with regard to university education—that all "sciences" were worthy of promotion, and that there was therefore no essential difference between the "old" and the "new" education; that religion had nothing to fear from science, and science need not be afraid of religion ("the interpreters may blunder, but truths are immutable, eternal, and never in conflict"); that in the promotion of science "remote utility" was quite as worthy to be thought of as immediate advantage; that no university could encourage with equal freedom all branches of learning, and that therefore a selection must be made in accordance with the requirements and deficiencies of a given people

[23] "And now I have this remarkable statement to make to you; that, without the least conference between us three, we all wrote letters telling them that the one man was Daniel C. Gilman of California. That is one of the few acts of my life which I have never regretted." (President Angell, of Michigan, at the twenty-fifth anniversary of Johns Hopkins University, 1902.)

at a given period. Likewise, the president believed, "individual students cannot pursue all branches of learning," and consequently they must be allowed to select, under the guidance of those appointed to counsel them, the fields of knowledge they were to explore. "Nor can able professors be governed by routine," said Gilman. "Teachers and pupils must be allowed great freedom in their methods of work. Recitations, lectures, examinations, laboratories, libraries, field exercises, travel, are all legitimate means of culture."

Several other points President Gilman thought were definitely settled about university education—that the best scholars would almost invariably be "those who make special attainments on the foundation of a broad and liberal culture"; that the best teachers would usually be those who were free, competent, and willing to make original researches in the library and the laboratory, and that the best investigators were usually those who have also the responsibilities of instruction, "gaining thus the incitement of colleagues, the encouragement of pupils, the observation of the public"; that universities should bestow their honors with a sparing hand, their benefits most freely. President Gilman thought, moreover, that the evidence was clear that "a university cannot be created in a day," that it is a slow growth; that universities easily fall into ruts, and almost any epoch requires a fresh start; that the ultimate object of the university is to develop character—to make men:

> It misses its aim if it produces learned pedants, or simple artisans, or cunning sophists, or pretentious practitioners. Its purport is not so much to impart knowledge to the pupils, as to whet the appetite, exhibit methods, develop powers, strengthen judgment, and invigorate the intellectual and moral forces. It should prepare for the service of society a class of students who will be wise, thoughtful, progressive guides in whatever department of work or thought they may be engaged.

On one point the president was particularly definite: "In forming all these plans we must beware lest we are led away from our foundations; lest we make our schools technical instead of liberal and impart a knowledge of methods rather than of principles. If we make this mistake we may have an excellent *Polytechnicum*, but not a *university*."

MEETING THE NEEDS OF THE DAY

One of the elements in the success of the Johns Hopkins University was the direct and immediate contribution it made to the higher education of the time. President Gilman was particularly alive to contemporary needs. Like Andrew D. White, he expected the American university, notwithstanding its British and continental derivations, to be different—to have work, for example, in American history and social and economic fields. As a partisan of the "new education," Gilman was never greatly bothered by whether the particular field of knowledge under consideration was an established one or not. He wrote in a letter from Geneva in August, 1875—a year before the University opened: "It has often seemed to me desirable that one of the specialties of the Johns Hopkins University should be the training up of young men to be the surveyors and engineers by whose skill our interior country will be mapped—the topographical, geological, agricultural and economical aspects."[24]

Gilman believed in the direct application of university teaching and research to the needs of everyday community life. He saw a close connection between the active kind of teaching and learning inherent in the newer higher education of his day and the larger needs of society. "What is the significance of all this activity?" he asked, and answered:

> It is reaching out for a better state of society than now exists; it is a dim but an indelible impression of the value of learning; it is a craving for intellectual and moral growth; it is a longing to interpret the laws of creation; it means a wish for less misery among the poor, less ignorance in schools, less bigotry in the temple, less suffering in the hospital, less fraud in business, less folly in politics; it means more study of nature, more love of art, more lessons from history, more security in property, more health in cities, more virtue in the country, more wisdom in legislation, more intelligence, more happiness, more religion.[25]

Science and the Modern Humanities

The plan was to begin with "those things that are fundamental and move gradually forward to those which are accessory." President Gilman recommended as first in order of importance of the newer fields of knowledge *Medical science* and *Biology* ("man in relation to nature") because at the time at which he spoke "in some of our very best colleges the degree of M.D. can be won in half the time required to win a degree of B.A." The president urged for the new university that great prominence should be given to studies which bear upon life—the biological sciences. He urged also what he called the *modern humanities*—

[24] Fabian Franklin, *Life of Daniel Coit Gilman*, pp. 202–203.
[25] From President Gilman's inaugural address.

The study of man in his relations to society, history, jurisprudence, political economy, legislation, taxation, finance, crime, pauperism, municipal government, morality in public and private affairs, "history of civilization and requirements of a modern state," national surveys and physical research, geodetical, topographical, meteorological, geological, zoological, botanical, economical—hence a department of physical research.

He was prepared to answer realistically, as a few words in his personal notebook show, the usual question about professional education: "Shall professional study be allowed?" He wrote: "Yes, renew the old faculties, but there is good reason in law and medicine for domesticating the professional study in a place of genial culture, under humanizing and liberalizing influences."

Dr. Gilman also had a place in his advanced university for "education" as a field of knowledge. "I can hardly doubt," he said, "that such arrangements as we are maturing will cause this institution to be a place for the training of professors and teachers for the highest academic posts; and I hope in time to see arrangements made for the unfolding of the philosophy, principles, and methods of education in a way which will be of service to those who mean to devote their lives to the highest departments of instruction." A decade later, when Dr. James Carey Thomas, a member of the board of trustees, was giving an account of the kind of university courses that had been introduced at the university, he listed not only offerings in the more usual literary, historical, and scientific fields, but also graduate courses in "Psychology, Pedagogics, and Philosophy; Mental Hygiene and Ethics."

The Denominational Question

Part of the need Gilman, Andrew D. White, Eliot, and others of their day had to meet was to develop a type of higher education that should have all the substantial character objectives of institutions under religious auspices and yet take its start from the newer scientific understanding of the times. It is difficult for us today to conceive of the extent to which denominational questions entered into higher education. By the time President Butler came to discuss the matter in his Columbia University reports in the 1900 period it was possible to do so with considerable objectivity, but the writings of both Gilman and White clearly indicate how intensely emotional a question this was, how important it was felt to be for advances in higher education. The new men, especially those concerned with building up State-supported universities like Cornell, were seriously perturbed over the opposition from the various denominational groups that had previously been chiefly responsible for higher education.[26] Mr. White said in one of his earliest published articles: "From the days when Henry Dunster, the first president of Harvard College, a devoted scholar and learned man, was driven from his seat with ignominy and cruelty (as Cotton Mather said afterward, he had 'fallen into the briars of antipedobaptism'), the sectarian spirit has been the worst foe of advanced education."[27] It should be made clear that Gilman was not opposed to the religious influence; he took an active part in encouraging religious institutions, but he feared the results of sectarian control on the newer sciences in the universities.[28]

A Selected Student Body

The unusual care exercised in selecting students for the university has already been mentioned. It would be hard to overestimate the value of this part of the plan. Twenty "Fellows" were appointed annually and there seems to have been unusually good selection. Apparently Dr. Gilman was able, with his wide acquaintance among college and university people, to attract the best men informed faculty persons could suggest. Of the sixty-nine persons admitted to the degree of Doctor of Philosophy in the first ten years for proficiency in various lines of special graduate study, either in letters or in science, fifty-six obtained positions as professors and teachers in thirty-two universities and colleges. To look through the list of first students at the Johns Hopkins University is to obtain a preview of the men who were to become the distinguished members of the faculties of American universities in the thirty or forty years that followed. Men now living who were students at Harvard or Columbia at the turn of the century would see name after name of the great men of their day in college. Whether they had been undergraduate or graduate students in universities of the type of these two at the period from 1900–1910, they would realize that an unusual proportion of the distinguished men they knew in their student days had been connected with the Johns Hopkins in some capacity—as teacher, university

---

[26] "One of the most prominent arguments against a State literary institution is that in time it will become infidel or sectarian." Thomas H. Benton, Jr. Address delivered at the Annual Commencement of the State University of Iowa, June 21, 1867. Having thus stated the argument Mr. Benton proceeded to answer it.

[27] Andrew D. White, *The Relation of the National and State Government to Advanced Education*, paper before the National Education Association, 1874.

[28] President Gilman established a voluntary chapel service at Hopkins, stipulating that no penalties or awards should be invoked for attendance or non-attendance. Miss Elisabeth Gilman states that her father always maintained an affiliation with the college chapel at Yale. He also served as president of the American Bible Society.

scholar, fellow, associate, or lecturer. A glance down the list of Fellows reveals names like these: Cyrus Adler, Maurice Bloomfield, William H. Burnham, J. McKeen Cattell, William H. Carpenter, Benjamin Ives Gilman, James Taft Hatfield, H. C. G. von Jageman, Charles R. Lanman, Marion D. Learned, Walter H. Page, Herbert Weir Smyth, William C. Thayer, Joseph S. Ames, Charles Lane Poor, John H. Latané, Josiah Royce, Bernard C. Steiner, W. W. Willoughby, Woodrow Wilson, Herbert B. Adams, John Spencer Bassett, John Dewey.

Numbers remained small. At no time in the first ten years did the matriculates (undergraduates) number one hundred. In 1885–86 there were 184 graduate students, ninety-six matriculates, and thirty-four specials. In 1895 there were 589 students, of whom 412 were graduates. The total for the first year of the university was eighty-nine. As late as 1903 only 163 were enrolled in the undergraduate courses, while "189 pursued graduated courses under the philosophical faculty, and 344 under the medical faculty."[29]

Absence of Prizes and Marks

Other than scholarships, no prizes of any kind were awarded, and there was no formal announcement of the comparative standing of students. "The students generally, undergraduates as well as graduates, do not require the stimulus of comparative marks and competitive examinations."

No special machinery was set up in the early days for admission to either undergraduate or graduate work. One of the first official circulars stated that three classes of students would be admitted: (a) matriculants, or candidates for a degree; (b) non-matriculants, not candidates for a degree, and devoted to a specialty like chemistry, biology, or engineering; (c) attendants upon separate courses of lectures, "whose names will not be enrolled among the students of the University"; and it was further added that "students in any of these groups must satisfy the authorities that they are mature enough in age, character, and acquisitions, to pursue with advantage the special advanced instruction here provided."[30]

Whatever results were obtained, especially with the advanced students, were very largely a matter of personal selection. Gilman himself had a wide acquaintance in university circles, and his friends in other institutions as well as in his own faculty kept their eyes open for promising men for the Hopkins opportunity. That Gilman would have been willing to travel across

[29] *New International Encyclopedia*, vol. XI, 1905, p. 256. (Article prepared under Gilman's editorship.)

[30] A number of students, especially from Baltimore, would attend courses for a considerable period and then "matriculate" later.

the continent to make sure of a man of original talent for one of his fellow-ships is the testimony of men still living who were closely identified with the beginnings of Johns Hopkins. "President Gilman's acquaintance among young men of promise in his day was such," writes Professor Charles R. Lanman, of Harvard University, "that one may safely set his success down as due in largest measure to his personal gift, in seeing youthful ability and rightly appraising it."[31] There were so few students at Johns Hopkins in his day, another distinguished Hopkins alumnus writes, that they did not have to be "handled" and "appraised" in any definite and regular fashion. He points out that the institution was in the highest degree informal, the in-formality applying both to relations between members of the faculty and relations with members of the student body, graduate and undergraduate. He adds:

> Undergraduate students were admitted by examination, but the distin-guishing feature was the elasticity with which these examinations were administered. I myself made a bad showing in mathematics, Latin, and Greek, but I had brought from a former Hopkins graduate a letter which told not only about me, but my family and their circumstances and the way in which we had struggled for an education, and I was frankly told that, though my papers were poor, Sale's letters showed that I was made of the right stuff. Not only was I admitted by Professor Morris, who was collegiate professor of Greek, but he himself guided me daily in making up my deficiencies in Greek. So did Professor Fabian Franklin in mathe-matics. . . .
>
> The air of informality which pervaded the undergraduates' work was also strong in the upper regions.

A Selected Faculty

In selecting both students and faculty, President Gilman never allowed himself or others connected with the University to forget that a university was made possible by human beings rather than by buildings. He knew, President Butler says, that "for a hospital you had to have a building," and so the hospital was built, but that for a university "you had to have men," and Gilman went out after the men. His selections for the first faculty have

---

[31] In a letter of November 18, 1937. See also, for some delightful recollections of the early days at Baltimore, Professor Lanman's "Living Reminiscences of Two or Three Generations Ago," an informal talk before the American Philosophical Society at Philadelphia, April 24, 1937. "Of President Gilman's 'First Twenty Fellows' of 1876, Ernest Sihler and I survive," Professor Lanman said in the course of his remarks.

On this point of personal selection, President Isaiah Bowman states that after the first few years "the correspondence shows a growing dependence upon the judgment of other men."

already been mentioned. Addressing the University in 1890 at the beginning of its fifteenth academic year, the President said:

> Whatever gains we make in our material condition, whatever limitations are still obvious, let us never forget, my friends, that men and methods make universities, not halls, nor books, nor instruments, important as these are. We cannot flatter ourselves that the large number of students who came here last year (almost the largest ever enrolled) nor the numbers now here were attracted by our architecture any more than by our victories on the athletic field. Let us rather believe that they were drawn here by the reputation of the teachers as men of learning and talent, scholars and investigators, and by expectations that the methods of instruction here employed would be stimulating, inspiring, and strengthening; that a strong personal interest would be shown in every student; that the companionship of scholars brought together from every part of the land, with diverse tastes, attainments, and tendencies would make an intellectual microcosm in which it would be profitable to dwell.

Gilman's flair for good teachers and his energy in going after them enhanced the difficulties of at least one other university of his day that was seeking superior faculty members. According to President Eliot's biographer, teaching positions at Harvard that up to this time had enjoyed a unique power of attraction no longer made the same appeal, because of the Hopkins. "In the end Gilman and Johns Hopkins raised up teachers for Harvard, but for a while it was their competition that was felt at Cambridge."[32]

A graduate student from North Carolina, when asked what he had found at Johns Hopkins that was most valuable, replied: "The freedom of access to able teachers and the stimulant of studying in company with men of maturer minds than one meets elsewhere." In later years it was to the faculty and its ability to work together that President Gilman attributed a large part of the achievement of the Johns Hopkins University. "The first requisite to success in any institution," he said, "is a body of professors, each of whom gives freely the best of which he is capable."

FREEDOM OF TEACHING AND LEARNING

In all his plans for the Johns Hopkins, Gilman had visioned a faculty free to teach and carry on research, and a student body correspondingly unrestricted. A personal notebook of 1876 contains a quotation from Goldwin Smith on how a university can best promote learning, "by allowing its

[32] Henry James, *Charles William Eliot*, vol. II, p. 14.

teachers, especially holders of great professorial chairs, liberal margin for private study." It was part of Gilman's thesis that, in the kind of university the Johns Hopkins was trying to be, the faculty would of necessity be made up of men for whom liberty of teaching and research was imperative. The enterprise sought to be, as President Butler of Columbia later testified from first-hand experience, a university in the real sense of the term—"universitas magistrorum et scholarium," a body of teachers and scholars.

"If our leader had been meddlesome, narrow-minded, unsympathetic, without tact, and dictatorial, our work could not have flourished," Dr. Remsen said later. Gilman was, Dr. Remsen went on to say, broad-minded to a remarkable degree, sympathetic, possessing confidence in those he had brought together, tactful and gentle even when harsh treatment appeared to be justified, as was sometimes the case. "He created an atmosphere good to live in—an atmosphere salutary and stimulating."[33]

Not, of course, that conditions were always ideal. There were difficult personalities, there were tensions; but the pettiness was somehow submerged in larger things.

Such was the informality in respect to the machinery of university organization that an able young student could, as Abraham Flexner did in his student days, enroll in more than one course scheduled for the same hour and not have it noticed until the examination schedule rolled around. The university register of the period shows that Flexner registered at the 1885 term in twelve courses—in Greek and Latin authors, French and German languages, comparative philology, logic, elocution, and drawing,—some of which clearly conflicted in the schedule.

J. B. Whitehead has recently given a picture of Johns Hopkins in the late 'eighties that helps to visualize what was going on at the University at a period when teachers were still more important than physical plant, though the plant had improved:

> In October, 1889, a seventeen-year old freshman entered the undergraduate elective group of historical-political courses leading in three years to the A.B. degree. . . . His entrance German absolved for him "German I" in the normal curriculum and necessitated the substitution of another course.
>
> It so happened that "Physics I" was the only possibility in his schedule, and thus he entered the course under Professor A. L. Kimball in the lecture room and Associate J. S. Ames in the laboratory, all within the new phys-

---

[33] In *Daniel Coit Gilman, First President of the Johns Hopkins University*, Johns Hopkins University circular, December, 1908.

ical laboratory building opened only two years earlier. The surroundings and equipment, the type of work in progress and particularly the personalities of the teaching staff and advanced students, were a revelation to our freshman. He remembers his many excursions, often unauthorized, into hidden and remote rooms from attic to basement of the Laboratory. Rowland was then in the full flight of his work on the solar spectrum, the mechanical equivalent of heat, the determination of the ohm, the magnetic effect of a moving charge, and other famous investigations. But he was also deeply interested in the applications of electricity and magnetism. In those days the incandescent lamp was still new, dynamo-electric machines in their most rudimentary stage of development, and neither measuring instruments nor motors available for the new and suspicious alternating current system. . . . Contact, even remote, with these activities, and early vision of an intimate relationship and community of interest between pure research and the applications of scientific knowledge, did something to our freshman which caused him to go early in the year to his adviser, Professor Herbert B. Adams, to arrange for a change of course in the next year so that he might prepare for admission as candidate for the certificate of Proficient in Applied Electricity.[34]

The method of the "seminary," or seminar, illustrates what in its beginnings must have been a refreshingly different way in university education. The earliest of the seminaries, as President Gilman told the story later, was, it happened, devoted to the study of Greek, but much the same method was followed in subsequent years in other fields:

Every day through the academic year the professor of Greek has been accustomed to meet a group of twenty or thirty college graduates, seated round a table, at the head of which his chair was placed, in the presence of the books which pertained to the particular author that was under discussion, and in close proximity to a library to which the class at other hours had the freest access. Each year a different subject was taken up. . . . Sometimes by a lecture, sometimes by questioning, sometimes by current comment, sometimes by the production of essays, the study was carried forward.[35]

C. S. Peirce must have had Johns Hopkins in mind when he wrote later that "modern scientists have been successful because they have spent their lives not in their libraries and museums but in their laboratories and in the field," and that the motive for doing this was "a craving to know how things really were, and an interest in finding out whether or not general propositions

[34] *The Johns Hopkins Alumni Magazine*, June, 1937, pp. 324–325.

[35] From the twentieth annual report of the President of the Johns Hopkins University.

actually held good—which has overbalanced all prejudice, all vanity, and all passion."[36] Five of the eight years that comprised Peirce's teaching period were spent at the Hopkins, where he was a lecturer on logic from 1879 to 1884. Baltimore was probably one of the few places where Peirce could have taught, for, while he was, his biographer says, "an inspiring teacher," he was too advanced for the ordinary student, having "a love of precision that made it impossible for him to make a popular appeal," and lacking capacity for making himself clear to large numbers. It was for the abler young students of the kind Johns Hopkins had that he was "a vital formative force, treating them as intellectual equals and impressing them as having a profound knowledge of his subject." He had only a small class of students in logic at Johns Hopkins, but four of them are credited with having made lasting contributions to the subject in a book which he edited and to which they contributed—*Studies in Logic*, 1883.[37]

It was in freedom of thinking and teaching, insisted upon from the start, that Dr. S. C. Mitchell found the "chief transmuting cause" for the change wrought between the previous activities of the members of the Johns Hopkins faculty and the "creative" character of their efforts in Baltimore. He pays tribute to the coordinating mind of Gilman himself, the emphasis upon advanced work with students already graduated from college, but in the main, he says, "this condition constituted the springtime that called forth in the Johns Hopkins group all the creative energies of their minds and methods. Exhilaration was in the very atmosphere."[38] Something of the same sort was in the mind of Professor Josiah Royce, the philosopher, when he said: "The beginning of the Johns Hopkins University was a dawn wherein ''twas bliss to be alive.' Freedom and wise counsel one enjoyed together. The air was full of noteworthy work done by the older men of the place, and of hopes that one might find a way to get a little working-power one's self. . . . One longed to be a doer of the word, and not a hearer only, a creator of his own infinitesimal fraction of a product, bound in God's name to produce it when the time came."[39]

"At Baltimore I was allowed almost absolute freedom to teach not only as, but what I could," wrote G. Stanley Hall many years later. He spoke par-

[36] Charles Sanders Peirce, *Collected Papers*, Cambridge, Harvard University Press, 1931, vol. I, p. 14.

[37] "Charles Sanders Peirce," *Dictionary of American Biography*, New York, Charles Scribner's Sons, 1934, vol. XIV, p. 398.

[38] *Dictionary of American Biography*, vol. VII, p. 301.

[39] Josiah Royce, "Present Ideals of American University Life," *Scribner's Magazine*, September, 1891, vol. X, no. 3, p. 383.

ticularly of Gilman as an "inside" president, whose interest in the work of the individual members of his faculty "did not end when they were engaged, but began":

> He loved to know something of their every new investigation, however remote from his own specialty, and every scientific or scholarly success felt the stimulus of his sympathy. His unerring judgment of men was triumphantly justified in the achievements of those he appointed; and although in selecting young men he had to walk by faith, he nowhere showed more sagacity than in applying individual stimuli and checks, so that in this sense and to this extent he was a spiritual father of many of his faculty, the author of their careers, and for years made the institution the paradise and seminarium of young specialists. This made stagnation impossible, and the growth of professors there in their work was, I believe, without precedent.[40]

Effect on Other Universities

Younger scholars at other universities (and some veterans as well) were pleased with the encouragement given by the president to scholarly work by the faculty. One of the younger members of the Harvard staff, when asked by President Eliot in 1881 to contribute toward a solution of the problem of "making the college an intellectual power in the country," wrote bluntly that one way would be for those in charge of the university at Cambridge to show something of the same interest that was shown to promising men and their work at Baltimore. "I have known intimately a considerable number of men who have been connected with the J. H. U.," wrote this young instructor, "and their testimony is unanimous as to the quick and general sympathy extended to every scholarly effort." Professor Child, who declined an invitation to leave Harvard and come to Johns Hopkins, nevertheless wrote to Gilman that the Johns Hopkins invitation had "helped him as well as pleased him because it had led to his being wholly relieved at last from the burden of correcting undergraduate compositions," so that he could proceed with his Chaucerian studies and his researches in ballad literature.[41]

That the freedom of teaching and learning referred to by Hall and others had its limitations, and was bound by certain laws, did not interfere with its operating effectively over many years at Baltimore. The two limitations Gilman insisted upon particularly were, first, that before students won the

[40] G. Stanley Hall, *Life and Confessions of a Psychologist*, New York, D. Appleton and Company, 1927, pp. 246–247.

[41] Henry James, *Charles William Eliot*, vol. II, p. 15.

privilege of independent study they must have been matured by "laborious and persistent pursuit of fundamental knowledge," and second, that the members of the faculty should understand that "with unselfish devotion to the discovery and advancement of truth and righteousness, they renounce all other preferment, so that, like the greatest of all teachers, they may promote the good of mankind."[42] Whatever "college" teachers might be (and Gilman had a rather limited notion of their possibilities), university teachers were ideally men who "have a gift for investigation, who are acute in suggesting important questions to be settled, and ingenious in devising the proper methods of solution—who delight to apply the touchstone of truth to every doctrine, and to carry the light of modern science into every field."

The Visiting Lecturer Plan

"Universities easily fall into ruts," President Gilman had reminded his hearers at the inaugural; "almost any epoch requires a fresh start."

One of the ways by which the president sought to overcome this weakness of educational institutions and at the same time make his instructional resources go as far as possible was the visiting lecturer plan. With $60,000 available for instruction the first year Gilman realized that he could hardly be expected to appoint a large staff of experienced teachers. To the "few leaders in the main departments of study" already described and a "promising group of associates or holders of fellowships" he could, however, add a "company of non-resident professors and lecturers," and this he undertook with a thoroughness that has probably never been equalled.

Gilman attributed the idea embodied in the Johns Hopkins outside lecture plan to Professor Benjamin Pierce, at Cambridge, who had recommended that "various colleges should send up for a portion of the year, and for a term of years, their best professors, who should receive a generous acknowledgment for this service, and good opportunities for work, but should not renounce their college homes."

"We have been fortunate in our guests," Gilman afterward wrote. They were. Huxley in a sense started it off with his address at the opening, but a long line of distinguished men followed him, sometimes for single lectures or short series, often for a period sufficiently long to make the lecturer in a real sense a part of the university, affecting students and the community as well. Gilman has told how the program of community lectures was set going the first year:

[42] From President Gilman's inaugural address.

The winter of 1876–77 was memorable in Baltimore. It was an era of good feeling—of great expectations. The differences of the Civil War were not forgotten, but they received no emphasis. The new foundation was welcomed as an agency of conciliation. . . .

In order to illustrate the activities of other universities, and to secure the counsel of eminent scholars in respect to our development, the decision had been reached already that academic lectures on various important and attractive themes should be opened to the public, and that the professors should come from institutions of acknowledged merit established in the North, South, and West. The usages of the Collège de France were in mind. Thus the instructions of a small faculty were to be supplemented by courses which should be profitable to the enrolled students, and entertaining, if not serviceable, to the educated public.[43]

President Gilman estimated later that in the first twenty-five years there must have been some three hundred of these lecturers and speakers from the outside. "Judge Cooley, the constitutional lawyer, the distinguished jurist, came from the great State University of Michigan, and Allen, the classical historian, from a kindred institution in Wisconsin. Harvard loaned us its two leading men of letters, Child and Lowell. Whitney, then at the height of his renown, came from Yale, and likewise Francis A. Walker. Hilgard and Billings represented the scientific activities of Washington—the former chosen because of his experience in geodesy, and because of our desire, at that early day, to initiate surveys in the State of Maryland; and the latter, because of his acknowledged distinction in medicine, which was soon to be a leading department of study among us. Simon Newcomb, the illustrious astronomer, was another man of science in the service of the government."

A course usually included twenty lectures. The lectures were given in a hall that held about 150 persons, and the hour was generally five o'clock. Ladies and gentlemen attended, without enrollment or fees, as well as the students and professors of the University. The lecturers were accessible to all who wished to confer with them. "Many among us formed friendships which lasted until the ties were severed by death. Sometimes bright students were spotted by these visiting professors, and afterward invited to positions of usefulness and distinction elsewhere—three at least to Harvard."

It was through this outside lecture plan that Thorstein Veblen, for example, came to know Charles Peirce, and discovered him to be "a creative

[43] Daniel Coit Gilman, *The Launching of a University*, pp. 60–62.

intellectual force," whose thinking constituted a radical departure from the "method of authority."[44]

Between 1877 and 1881 the principal lecturers ("engaged for such long periods that they could not properly be called non-resident"), were Francis J. Child, English literature; James Russell Lowell, Romance literature; Francis A. Walker, political economy; William James, psychology; Hermann von Holst, history; Sidney Lanier, English literature; Charles S. Peirce, logic; John Trowbridge, physics; A. Graham Bell, phonology; S. P. Langley, physics; James Bryce, political science.

Edward Ingle, a student of the period, has pictured, among others of the interesting visitors and lecturers of the early days:

> Sidney Lanier, exemplifying in the bodily feebleness that would not allow him to stand in delivering his lectures, the tragedy of his life, "Aspiro dum exspiro." . . .
>
> Hermann von Holst, spare of figure and of animated countenance, in brilliant exposition of European history. . . .
>
> Woodrow Wilson, reading to the Historical Seminary manuscript chapters of his *Congressional Government*. . . .
>
> Shosuke Sato, in masterly handling of American documents treating of the opening of Japan.
>
> Presidents Charles Eliot of Harvard and Andrew D. White of Cornell, manifesting by their presence their personal interest in the president in whose choice as the head of the university they had had a decided influence. . . .
>
> Samuel P. Langley, not yet blazing the way for the aeroplane, but calling James E. Keeler to be his assistant at the Allegheny Observatory.[45]

From the point of view of the new university it was properly held to be a great advantage to bring into an academic circle men from other universities—"observing, critical, suggestive, familiar with different ways, looking perhaps for colleagues or for assistants, asking help, answering questions, showing methods." Dr. Fabian Franklin has pointed out in his biography how important these outside lectures were to the beginnings of the University—"the element of richness and color, as well as of solid intellectual quality" they provided:

> Without the background of history, without the stimulus of comparison or rivalry with similar institutions, in an environment offering no sus-

---

[44] Joseph Dorfman, *Thorstein Veblen and his America*, New York, The Viking Press, 1934, p. 41.

[45] Edward Ingle, "The First Ten Years at Johns Hopkins," *The Johns Hopkins Alumni Magazine*, November, 1915, pp. 23–24.

tenance to the peculiar and specialized activities being carried on by little groups of workers, it requires no great effort to imagine the danger that there might be something arid or anaemic about the life of the Johns Hopkins University in its beginnings. As a matter of fact quite the opposite of all this actually characterized those early years, and it would be difficult to say in just what measure this happy result was brought about by that added touch of breadth and distinction which was given by the presence of men like Lowell and Child and Whitney and Newcomb and Cooley and Walker, and by the refreshing perspectives of great fields of thought which they and other non-resident and resident lecturers of the first two years placed before this little body of university pioneers and the cultivated public of Baltimore.

Somewhat similar to the outside-lecturer plan in its inter-university values was the large number of associates, readers, and assistants, "most such appointments having been made for brief periods among young men of promise looking forward to preferment in this institution or elsewhere." Some observers of the period, including Dr. Nicholas Murray Butler, have considered this almost as important as the more ambitious lecture program, not only because it helped strengthen the young university, but because it made its work known wherever scholarship was esteemed.

THE SCHOLARLY JOURNALS

The importance President Gilman attached to the right kind of scholarly journals is illustrated by the oft-repeated story of his discovery of Rowland, the physicist. In the summer of 1875 Gilman asked a friend at West Point who there was who could be considered for the chair of physics at the new university. This friend mentioned Rowland, then at the Rensselaer Polytechnic Institute, Troy, New York, as a young man full of promise who had recently published a significant article in the *Philosophical Magazine*. "Why did he publish it in London?" asked Gilman, "and not in the *American Journal?*" "Because it was turned down by the American editors," was the reply, "and the writer at once forwarded it to Professor Clerk Maxwell, who sent it to the English periodical." [46]

To the new university scientific and scholarly journals were essential. If the University was to produce anything in research there must be some way of making it known, for, as President Butler of Columbia said many years after in reviewing the Johns Hopkins venture, "through publication a uni-

[46] Daniel Coit Gilman, *The Launching of a University*, p. 15. Also cited in the article on Gilman in the *Dictionary of American Biography*, vol. VII, p. 301.

versity spreads abroad, for specialists and all who care to know, the results of the researches of its teachers and students, and so makes them, in the best sense, practical—that is, effective."[47] When President Gilman came to write his story in later years he explained that he had taken the idea of scholarly publications from Germany, and he remarked that they had proved to be "a noteworthy factor in the usefulness of the Johns Hopkins University."[48]

First of the Johns Hopkins periodicals in point of time was the *American Journal of Mathematics* (1878) with Sylvester as editor. Next came the *American Chemical Journal*, under Remsen (1879), and the *American Journal of Philology*, with Professor Gildersleeve in charge. The *American Chemical Journal* was started, Gilman states, when Professor Remsen and his students found it impossible to get publication for their chemistry contributions in the *American Journal of Science*. By 1886 the "Publication Agency" of the University, headed by Mr. Nicholas Murray, was concerned with six regular periodicals, the three already mentioned, and in addition, *Studies from the Biological Laboratory* (H. Newell Martin and W. K. Brooks); *Studies in Historical and Political Science* (Herbert B. Adams); and the *Johns Hopkins University Circular*. The "Agency" was also handling *Contributions to Logic*, edited by Charles S. Peirce, and was aiding in the publication of the *Journal of Physiology*, transferred from Cambridge, England, in 1881.[49] *Modern Language Notes* began appearing in April, 1886, with A. Marshall Elliott as managing editor and James W. Bright, Julius Goebel, and Henry A. Todd as associate editors. "The desire of the Editors," said the editorial in the first issue, "is to give to this little periodical as scientific a character as may be possible, considering the present status of modern language study in America."

The development of the *Circular* illustrates President Gilman's interest in promoting scholarship through every possible medium. Originally only an announcement of courses, the *Circular* was turned into a folio in 1879, with class lists, accounts of the activities of societies and seminaries, and abstracts of papers presented before these two types of organization. The societies proved to be significant for scholarship and scholarly publication. Beginning with semi-social monthly meetings at which papers were read, they soon took on a more serious function and had a semi-official standing

---

[47] *American Monthly Review of Reviews*, January, 1901, p. 52.

[48] Daniel Coit Gilman, *The Launching of a University*, p. 115.

[49] Edward Ingle, "The First Ten Years at Johns Hopkins," *The Johns Hopkins Alumni Magazine*, November, 1915, p. 13.

in the University. They included a general scientific association, a philological association (still in existence), an historical association, and a mathematical conference. Later there came a Metaphysical Club and a Naturalists' Field Club. The meetings of these societies were reported in the *Circular*, with abstracts of the more important papers, and some issues of the *Circular* also carried abstracts of the articles that had appeared in the more formal journals.[50]

Not only was the production of scholarly journals and other publications an essential part of the Johns Hopkins research program, but it also fitted in with the strong notion Gilman and his associates had as to the community responsibility of a university and the obligation resting on an institution of learning to meet ascertained public needs with the most effective use of combined resources. One of the four ways the president specifically approved for promoting learning on the part of a university was "by assisting through its university press in the publication of learned works which an ordinary publisher would not undertake."[51] He wanted wide publication even for discussions of university policy, giving prominence in his first annual report to a commendation of Harvard University for adopting a plan of public announcements of the action of its Board, and making clear that he expected to maintain a similar policy of publicity for Johns Hopkins: "The University cannot thrive unless it has the confidence of enlightened men, and this confidence can most readily be secured by that publicity which fully and regularly makes known the conclusions of the Trustees."

Moreover, he did not encourage the beginning of any periodical or publication unless there was a demonstrated need for it. He allowed the *American Journal of Mathematics* to start only when he found that a single periodical for the two sides of the Atlantic was not practicable. He kept constantly in mind possibilities of unconventional types of inter-university relationships, as in the plan of external lecturers and temporary associates previously described. The publication policy of the Johns Hopkins University was directly affected by the fact that a research library of 60,000 volumes was available in the nearby Peabody Institute.[52] From the beginning President Gilman had Johns Hopkins working for the kind of cooperation that sought

---

[50] This information on the *Circular* was furnished by Dr. John C. French, of the Library of the Johns Hopkins University. See also the *Third Annual Report*, p. 20.

[51] From a personal notebook in the Johns Hopkins University Library.

[52] Some present-day faculty members feel, however, that dependence upon Peabody Institute facilities handicapped library development later. For a statement of this point of view, see the article by Professor George Boas in the November, 1937, issue of the *Johns Hopkins Alumni Magazine*, p. 4.

to avoid rivalry with other institutions, to accept heartily all the assistance that could be secured from other foundations, and "to aid generously in promoting the advancement of the public welfare so far as it may depend upon university influences." [53]

---

[53] *Johns Hopkins University Register, 1880–81,* p. 21.

II

CLARK UNIVERSITY, A GRADUATE INSTITUTION

*All the refinements of the world seem now to take refuge
in the smaller things; the bigger ones are getting too
big for any virtue to remain with them. You have done
something original and succeeded perfectly.*

WILLIAM JAMES, letter to G. Stanley Hall on the
Clark University Decennial Celebration, 1899.

WHEN G. Stanley Hall left Johns Hopkins in 1888 to head the newly
created Clark University at Worcester, Massachusetts, it was with
the expectation of developing "a purely graduate institution" that would
carry out the original Johns Hopkins purposes even more substantially than
had been done at Baltimore.

"The epoch-making work of the Johns Hopkins University," Hall wrote
later, "had leavened the colleges and roused them from the life of monotony
and routine which then prevailed, and kindled a strong and widespread desire for better things. But financial clouds had already begun to threaten this
great Southern luminary, and there were indications that, if the great work
it had begun was to be carried on, parts of it, at least, must be transplanted
to new fields." With a dozen colleges within a radius of a hundred miles of
Worcester, the plainest logic of events, Hall maintained, was for Clark to
take the "inevitable next step" beyond Hopkins, eliminating "college work"
altogether, waiving the test of numbers, "selecting rigorously the best students, seeking to train leaders only, educating professors, and advancing
science by new discoveries."[1]

The president was to have a free hand. The founder and trustees, John
D. Washburn's letter of invitation said, "desire to impose on you no tram-
mels; they have no friends for whom they wish to provide at the expense of
the Institution; no pet theories to press upon you in derogation of your judgment; no sectarian tests to apply; no guarantees to require save such as are
implied by your acceptance of this trust."

Whatever questions were to arise later as to the function of the University,
President Hall did his best to make clear at the outset the specialized graduate opportunity he visioned for Clark. In his first report, drawn up immediately after his return from the European trip of 1888–89, he reiterated his
view that the "new movement" in higher education was in full swing in

---

[1] *Clark University, 1889–1899: Decennial Celebration*, Worcester, Clark University Press, 1899, p. 48.

America, and that Clark University's task was unmistakably defined thereby. The University must be "of the highest and most advanced grade, with special prominence given to original research." It must seek the most talented and best trained young men, for—

> We are not a "graduate department" in which most so-called graduate students attend and most professors conduct undergraduate work. . . . We are a school for professors, where leisure, method, and incentive train select men to higher and more productive efficiency than before.[2]

BEGINNINGS OF CLARK UNIVERSITY

Jonas Gilman Clark was an enterprising New Englander who had returned to his native Worcester County after business successes in California and elsewhere had made him a man of wealth. Born at Hubbardston, Massachusetts, in 1815, he spent his boyhood on the farm, getting limited schooling in the district school. At sixteen he was apprenticed to a wheelwright, and at twenty-one he set up in business for himself, entering early into the manufacture of chairs. Louis N. Wilson reports how, after working hard all day, young Clark would start out with a load of chairs for Boston, and, "on coming to a covered bridge he had to unload the top row of chairs, drive through the bridge, and then walk back and bring those chairs through the bridge and load them again."[3] Some years later Clark started the manufacturing of tinware. He succeeded so well that he sold out his carriage and chair departments and devoted himself to tinware, hardware, and building materials. In 1853 he began shipping miners' supplies and farm tools to California, and shortly after he and Mrs. Clark crossed the continent to San Francisco where Mr. Clark set up what proved to be a profitable business in wholesale furniture. He also bought land in and around the San Francisco Bay region which became very valuable. Clark was an active member of the Vigilantes; exercised considerable influence in the activities whereby California was kept in the Union during the early days of the Civil War; knew and esteemed Leland Stanford. His health failing in 1860, Clark wound up his California business, invested the proceeds in real estate, and went with Mrs. Clark on the first of a number of trips to Europe. After the Civil War he moved from California to New York, built a home in New York City, and invested still further in real estate, which he is reported to have sold in

---

[2] Clark University, *President's Report, 1890.*

[3] Louis N. Wilson, "Some Recollections of Our Founder," *Publications of Clark University Library,* vol. 8, no. 2, February, 1927, pp. 3 ff.

later years at a considerable profit. In 1879 he and Mrs. Clark returned to Worcester, where Mr. Clark built a residence and several large business blocks.

Friends of Mr. Clark describe him as having by this time developed an "impassioned interest" in books and bindings, in paintings and statuary:

> He collected choice manuscripts and incunabula; over 2,000 volumes in elegant bindings; several thousand books of history and travel, and over 100 pictures. The pictures and the rarer books now form the Clark Memorial Collection in our University Library. In his later years he was especially devoted to books, and showed this interest in a very practical way by giving the Clark Library a separate endowment, large enough to ensure its proper support.[4]

Others say of him that he was a rather lonely old man, desirous of entering, with his wife, into the social life of Worcester, but having little knowledge of how to go about it.

In the latter part of 1886 Mr. Clark invited a number of prominent citizens of Worcester, including United States Senator George F. Hoar and General Charles Devens, to serve with him on the Board of Trustees for a university which he proposed to found, and in March, 1887, Clark University received its charter from the General Court of Massachusetts.

What kind of university did Mr. Clark contemplate? Available evidence appears to bear out Louis N. Wilson's opinion, based on personal acquaintance and conversations with the founder during his lifetime, that Mr. Clark had in mind "an institution for the education of poor boys, who, for the sake of a collegiate education at a very low tuition, would be willing to forego the outward glories of the older universities." Wilson says:

> Perhaps he had visions of Commencement Days when, seated on the platform, he should look into the happy faces of parents gathered to see their boys receive their diplomas from his hands, and should feel that he had won their affection and their esteem. He would be a patron and benefactor, after the pattern of Europe; he would do good, and his name should be honored in the land. The sons of his fellow-citizens, less fortunate than he in material things, should by his means and under his guidance be introduced to the things of the mind, to the world of beauty and of intellectual values which he himself had so lately and so eagerly come to know. It was all very real and very sincere; but could the University, in Mr. Clark's thinking, have been much more than a glorified high school?[5]

[4] Ibid., p. 6.

[5] "Address of the Founder," May 4, 1887, *Publications of the Clark University Library*, vol. 8, no. 2,

In his address at the opening Mr. Clark had spoken somewhat generally of the aims of the new institution, but on one point he was clear and definite. "In proceeding with this work which we are about to undertake," he said, "the first step seems to be to plan and construct the necessary buildings, or, at least, a part of them. In anticipation of this part of our labors, I have prepared a plan or design which I present for your examination, and which will invite your criticism or commend itself to your approval, after having such explanation of it generally and in detail, as I am able to give." And he recommended "that we proceed at once and with all convenient dispatch to erect such building or buildings as may be found needed, and as may be required for the prosecution of a collegiate course, and have the same in such a state of forwardness that the first class may present itself for examination and admission on the first Monday of October in the year one thousand eight hundred and eighty-eight."

Unlike the Johns Hopkins, therefore, Clark was to begin with buildings— one or more university buildings designed for the purpose by the founder in advance of the coming of the educational leader to direct the enterprise.

PRESIDENT G. STANLEY HALL

The Clark Trustees selected for the presidency of the new institution Granville Stanley Hall, then professor at the Johns Hopkins University, of whom President Charles William Eliot was to say a few years later with characteristic conciseness:

> Eleven years after Granville Stanley Hall took his A.B. at Williams College, and seven years after he graduated at Union Theological Seminary, Harvard had the honor of conferring on him the Ph.D. earned by residence and examinations.
>
> The Harvard doctorate has never been more worthily bestowed or better illustrated in the subsequent career.[6]

Hall's preparation for the leadership of a great experiment in higher education differed from that of Daniel Coit Gilman, but in many respects it was no less thorough and distinguished. Hall and William James had both been under consideration for the opportunity at Johns Hopkins that had gone to Hall, and from the laboratory of experimental psychology estab-

February, 1927, pp. 16–19. It should not be inferred from this quotation that Mr. Clark was necessarily unsympathetic to the promotion of research and higher studies. For further discussion of this point see page 60.

[6] Letter of July 18, 1903, bound in a personal volume of testimonials to Dr. Hall, now in the possession of his son, Dr. Robert G. Hall, of Portland, Oregon.

lished at Baltimore (first of such laboratories in the United States and second in the world, Wilhelm Wundt's having been the first) students had already come forth who were to be outstanding leaders in experimental psychology and related fields for several generations—among them men as different in their attainments and interests as John Dewey, Joseph Jastrow, J. McKeen Cattell, and G. T. W. Patrick. Like Gilman, Hall had been in no hurry to settle down into an established educational position, and he had sampled the educational provisions of the day in a variety of experiences in this country and abroad. Unlike Gilman, he had had comparatively little to do with the administrative side of education, though in grasp of educational philosophy and brilliancy of presentation he was already far ahead of most of the men of his time.

Granville Stanley Hall was born at Ashfield, Massachusetts, February 1, 1844. On his father's side he was a descendant of Elder William Brewster, who came over in the *Mayflower*, John Lillie, and other founders of early Massachusetts families; through his mother he traced his ancestry to John and Priscilla Alden. He grew up in a family of "substantial, hardworking, comfortable, commonsense farmers" characterized by great physical vigor and extreme conservatism.[7] He received his early schooling in local district schools, spent a brief period at the Ashfield Academy, and after a year at Williston Academy, Easthampton, entered Williams College in 1863. After graduating from Williams in 1867 he went to Union Theological Seminary, New York City, teaching in a school for girls to help pay his way, attending every conceivable kind of dramatic performance then in vogue, making systematic visits to slum areas, and in other ways becoming acquainted at first hand with the various aspects of human life in a large city. Henry Ward Beecher, whose church he joined, advised young Hall, when he found him more interested in philosophy than theology, to go to Germany for further study, and even wrote a note to Henry W. Sage which resulted in Sage lending the money to make the trip possible.

Hall left New York for Germany in May, 1868. He studied first at Bonn, later at Berlin, had a brief contact with the Franco-Prussian War as newspaper correspondent, indulged his passion for the theater and the opera, and made several unsuccessful attempts to arrange for an opportunity to teach philosophy in some American college or university. He returned to New York

---

[7] "My grandfather, for instance, always preferred the slow-moving oxen for all kinds of farm work to horses. . . . These people were pretty set in the good old ways, and if they did make innovations or progress it was only in particular items and it was done with a great deal of self-consciousness." (G. Stanley Hall, *Life and Confessions of a Psychologist*, pp. 56–57.)

in 1871, completed his theological course there, and became resident tutor in the family of Jesse Seligman, the banker.

In 1872 Hall secured a teaching position at Antioch College, Ohio, where he spent four happy and profitable years. It was at Antioch, one of his biographers says, where Hall "probably acquired that affection for the lecture room which he retained to the end of his days."[8] He taught English literature the first year, became professor of modern languages the year following, and then took over the work in philosophy, making that subject his main interest for the remainder of his stay at Antioch. In addition to teaching, Hall "preached, was impresario for the college theater, chorister, conducted the rhetorical exercises, and 'spread out' generally." He did a great deal of solid reading in the Antioch period, however, he afterward insisted, and when Wilhelm Wundt's *Grundzüge der physiologischen Psychologie* appeared in 1874 Hall became so deeply interested in it that he determined to return to Germany and enter Wundt's laboratory. When he came East in 1876 to carry out this plan, President Eliot of Harvard offered him a position as college tutor in English at a salary of $1,000 under Professors Child and Hill, and Hall felt obliged to accept the offer. He remained two years, though he found the work at Cambridge "very monotonous after the freer air at Antioch."[9] He took his doctor's degree at Harvard at the end of this two-year period and left immediately after Commencement for his second trip to Germany. Hall's own description of his stay at Berlin not only gives an interesting picture of the educational opportunities that attracted American students to German universities during this era but also shows something of the stage of development Hall himself had reached by this time:

The period of my stay abroad was one when academic traditions in Germany favored more general and less acutely special studies than now. Indeed, in these delightful years, there was almost no limit to the field over which a curious student, especially if he was not working for a degree, might roam. He could indulge his most desultory intellectual inclinations, taste at any spring, and touch any topic in the most superficial way in his

[8] Louis N. Wilson, "Biographical Sketch," *Granville Stanley Hall, February 1, 1844–April 24, 1924, In Memoriam. Publications of the Clark University Library*, vol. 7, no. 6, May, 1925, p. 18. The brief account of Hall's life here given is based on Wilson's material and on H. D. Sheldon's article on Hall in the *Dictionary of American Biography*, vol. VIII, pp. 127–130.

[9] "He had the sophomore class, of about 250, in three divisions, reciting an hour each from 9 to 12 each morning, repeating the required lesson. It was almost the only required course and was, therefore, hated by the students. He also had to correct the two three-hour examination papers of each of his 250 students, besides the four 'sprung' one-hour written 'exams' and the six themes required of each." (Louis N. Wilson, "Biographical Sketch," pp. 20–24.)

effort to orient himself. He could take the widest periscope, and, especially if an American, he was allowed to drop into almost anything to his heart's content, so that there were others besides myself who yielded to the charm of spending much of each day in the lecture rooms, hearing often very elaborate experimental and demonstrational introductory courses, most of them five hours a week. Fresh from the narrow, formal, rather dry curriculum of a denominational American college, the stimulus and exhilaration of this liberty of hearing was great. During the first triennium, besides the more stated work, I took the complete course of Dorner in theology, translating my notes afterward, attended Trendelenburg's seminary on Aristotle, heard Delitzsch's biblical psychology, logical courses by Lasson, recent psychology by Pfleiderer, comparative religion by Lazarus. I even tried to follow the venerable Hegelian Michelet, Drobisch, the Nestor, and Strümpell, the more poetic expositor of Herbartianism, and took Kirchmann's courses. I heard much more of these men in the weekly philosophical club, and dropped in occasionally to about all the courses that my friends among the students were taking. Even in the second triennium this *Wanderlust* was not extinct. I attended full courses each in chemistry by Kolbe, biology by Leuckart, physiology by Du Bois-Reymond at Berlin, and Ludwig at Leipzig, anatomy by His, neurology by Flechsig, Westphal's clinic at the Charité, running over later to Paris for a month to get a glimpse of Charcot's work there, and to Vienna to sample Meynert and Exner. Virchow and Bastian were both lecturing in anthropology. Indeed, we students "dropped in" to almost everything—clinics, seminary, laboratory, lecture—and if we had a goodly number of registrations in our book, we were practically unmolested wherever we went. Perhaps all this meant more distraction than concentration, but if it was mental dissipation, it at any rate left a certain charm in memory and brought a great and sudden revelation of the magnitude of the field of science.[10]

Shortly after Dr. Hall returned from Europe in 1880, "again in the depths because of debt and with no prospects," President Eliot rode up to the small flat on the edge of Somerville where the Halls were living, rapped on the door without dismounting from his horse, and asked Hall to begin Saturday of that week a course of lectures on pedagogy in Boston under the auspices of Harvard University. The University was to assume the expense of the hall, pay for printing, and advertise the course. President Eliot agreed to introduce Hall at the first lecture; this he did by stating that Harvard had never been much impressed by pedagogy, but that Dr. Hall was "a

[10] G. Stanley Hall, *Founders of Modern Psychology*, New York, D. Appleton and Company, 1912, pp. vi–vii. Given also in Louis N. Wilson's *G. Stanley Hall*, New York, G. E. Stechert, 1914, pp. 43–44, and in his "Biographical Sketch," pp. 23–24.

young man who had studied it abroad and this course had been instituted as an experiment."[11] So successful were the lectures that Hall was invited to give the series again the following year.

In 1882 President Gilman offered Dr. Hall a lectureship in psychology at the Johns Hopkins University with an appropriation of $1,000 a year for building up a psychological laboratory. In 1884 he was made professor of psychology and pedagogics, lecturing on psychology, graduate and undergraduate; psychologic and ethical theories; physiological psychology; history of philosophy and education. He gave many of the outside public lectures that were a feature of the Hopkins program of that day, and in 1887, through the interest of a gentleman who had heard him lecture in Philadelphia, was enabled to carry out an ambition he had long cherished and begin the issuing of a journal devoted to the new psychology—the *American Journal of Psychology*. He was thus well established in one of the most significant educational enterprises of his day.

Invitation to Clark

Just how Dr. Hall's name first came to be mentioned in connection with Clark University is not known, but Senator Hoar, who had previously met Hall in both Worcester and Washington, broached the matter to him early in 1888, and within a very short time afterward Mr. Clark himself, Senator Hoar, and John D. Washburn, secretary of the Clark Trustees, called upon Dr. Hall at his home in Baltimore. A visit to Mr. Clark's house in Worcester followed, and the official notice of election was mailed on April 3, 1888.

Hall hesitated before finally deciding to leave Hopkins for the new post. He was, as he informed Mr. Washburn, "absorbed in a department of academic work which is new and full of promise, and attached by strong official and personal ties to an institution where the stimulus to research is strong and the enthusiasm for science is great—where much has already been done and the hope of future achievement is high." He could not be induced to leave Baltimore merely to organize another college of the traditional New England type, or even to duplicate those that were best among established institutions old or new, he wrote. But "the single and express desire that in whatever branches of sound learning it may engage, the new University may be a leader and a light," and the promise this held for progress in higher education in America, drew him to Clark with a hope and enthusiasm too strong to resist.

---

[11] G. Stanley Hall, *Life and Confessions of a Psychologist*, p. 217.

The letter of acceptance was sent in May, 1888. President Hall was at once granted a year's leave of absence and departed on a "pedagogic tour" which he himself characterized as "without precedent in the history of education." He had worked out an elaborate plan for interviewing leading men in science, visiting higher educational institutions, laboratories, libraries, and bookshops, investigating administrative methods, collecting as much pamphlet material as possible, and seeing instrument makers and securing apparatus for his own department of psychology. This program he carried out systematically, according to his own statements, and although he admitted disappointment in one of his chief quests—that of bringing to America two or three distinguished European scholars for the Clark faculty—he came back to Worcester "surcharged with academic idealism and with the very highest hopes and expectations." He was more than ever convinced that Clark had the opportunity to develop a type of advanced university work not hitherto attempted in the United States, even at Johns Hopkins.

THE FIRST THREE YEARS

Clark University opened in the fall of 1889 with a small group of advanced students—students who, Edmund C. Sanford said, were "hardly distinguishable in age or attainments from the younger instructors to whose lectures they listened." At the public opening exercises addresses were delivered by General Devens and Edward Everett Hale, and various announcements were made tending to emphasize the advanced nature of the work the University proposed to do. This was to be limited at the outset to five divisions: mathematics, physics, chemistry, biology, and psychology, with such additional facilities for the study of languages as scientific students might require. It was explained that "this preliminary limitation of the wide academic field indicates no bias and no restriction of ulterior plans, but is adopted in the interest of more effective organization." The University would accept various classes of students—"independent students," those who had already taken the doctorate or had had corresponding training and experience and were ready to go forward with particular lines of research ("docents"); candidates for the degree of doctor of philosophy; special students not candidates for degrees; medical students; and "preliminary candidates" who lacked only one year of a degree. It was the candidates for the doctor's degree, however, for whom the institution was really designed. "It is to the need of these students that the lectures, seminaries, laboratories and collections of books and apparatus will be especially shaped, and no pains will be spared to afford them every needed stimulus and opportunity." Fellowship and scholarship aid included thirty full tuitions at $200 each, with eight of these on fellowships at $400 per annum.

As at Johns Hopkins, special attention had been given to selection of both students and faculty, and the men who made up the Clark teaching and research group at its opening were the best possible indication of the intention to do scholarly work at an advanced level.

Unquestionably the new institution was off to a good start. The idea of a small, highly selective group of scholars and research workers working together in a new type of university foundation—new to the United States, at least—made an appeal. Although no one knew just what financial resources were going to be available, the beginnings were promising. Mr. Clark had put at the disposal of the institution, in addition to land and buildings, $600,000 for university endowment and $100,000 for the support and maintenance of the library—a modest sum as compared with later endowments, perhaps, but regarded then by the trustees and others as "the largest single charitable gift ever made by a private person in New England, and with very few exceptions the largest ever made by a private person all in a lifetime anywhere in the world." The interest on these amounts was at first supplemented by annual grants from Mr. Clark, so that actually the first year $135,000 was spent for salaries and equipment, the second year $92,000, the third year $68,000.

Faculty and Students

Even though these were, as will be noticed, declining amounts, it was possible to secure through them—especially with the selective skill of President Hall and the wide publicity given to the new venture—a superior faculty and student group. "Hall chose an extraordinarily gifted group of men," says E. L. Thorndike. The personnel that had been assembled during the first and second years included, at the head of the department of mathematics, W. E. Story, who had been associated with Hall in the faculty at Baltimore; Oskar Bolza, a scholar of German training; A. A. Michelson, already known for his measurement of light waves and later a Nobel prize winner; A. G. Webster, then a promising young physicist just home from four years of European study; Arthur Michael, professor of chemistry; J. U. Nef, later head of the department of chemistry at the University of Chicago; and C. O. Whitman, a pioneer in zoological work in America. Hall rightly says in his autobiography that the list of "fellows" and even "scholars" during these first two or three years contained the names of many who have since achieved eminence. Men now living who were at Clark in these early years still glow with enthusiasm when they tell about it. "Clark was a marvellous place," says President-emeritus William L. Bryan, of Indiana University, who went to Worcester in 1891 and was in a position to evaluate the work of the new university in comparison with Berlin and Johns Hopkins. "For a student in psychology there were, besides G. Stanley Hall himself, E. C. Sanford, an excellent research man; William H. Burnham, in education; H. H. Donaldson, the neurologist; Franz Boas, in anthropology; and Warren P. Lombard, in physiology. Hall had gone out to get the men, as Gilman had done at Hopkins, and he had been successful in bringing together a very superior faculty."[12] For a brief period, at least, Henry D. Sheldon says, "the university was received with wide acclaim and accomplished work of a high order."[13]

A Critical Situation

Trouble came in the third year. It is not pertinent to the present inquiry to analyze this in any detail, and certainly not to stir the embers of an ancient controversy. It is necessary, however, to try to secure a sufficient understanding of what happened to help answer the basic question in the present study; namely, What were the features of Clark University that account for its acknowledged success? It may perhaps prove to be of importance for our inquiry to discover that Clark made a distinguished contribution to education on the graduate level not only as the result of certain favorable elements but in spite of difficulties so critical that those in charge of the enterprise all but despaired of carrying on.

Of the seriousness of the situation that developed in the Worcester experiment there can be little question. "By the end of the third year," wrote Hall in his autobiography, "Clark seemed to many outsiders not unlike a derelict abandoned by most of its officers and crew, while to me it was a graveyard of high hopes and aspirations. The collapse of our great expectations and of the plans we thought so nearly ideal was mortifying and humiliating beyond the power of words to describe."[14]

What was it that had happened so unexpectedly as almost to destroy the new enterprise before it was fairly started? President Hall's own explanation, as given years later in the autobiography, was largely a financial one. He

[12] From an interview at Bloomington, Indiana, January 7, 1938.
[13] *Dictionary of American Biography*, vol. VIII, pp. 127–130.
[14] G. Stanley Hall, *Life and Confessions of a Psychologist*, pp. 5–6.

pointed out that Mr. Clark's supplementary grants for the University had decreased from $50,000 the second year to $12,000 the fourth, and then had ceased altogether. He says:

> Undoubtedly the University was costing more than he expected, students were fewer, and the income from their fees was practically nil. . . . The chief solicitude of the board and myself was focused upon Mr. Clark's resources and his immediate and subsequent intentions, but upon these topics he gave us no ray of light although repeatedly urged by the board, individually and collectively, to do so. He had sanctioned every engagement and knew exactly the liabilities we were incurring, and the optimistic view was that he could not possibly bring men here or start departments and then fail to sustain them. As he himself had encouraged us to commit ourselves to a budget so far in excess of our regular resources it was constantly hoped that additional permanent gifts from him would be forthcoming, so that when even his annual "donations" began to diminish there was hardly less than consternation in the board. When any question of reengagement occurred we had to consider carefully whether, in view of all the circumstances, it ought to be made at all, and some of our best appointees were dropped, when their terms expired, for no other cause.[15]

President Hall also mentions administrative difficulties arising out of Mr. Clark's direct interest in the everyday working of the University, natural enough, it would seem, on the part of a founder, but tending, the President felt, toward unwarranted interference with the professional direction of the institution. Mr. Clark had not only actively supervised the erection of the main university building—which was a copy of a building he had put up in downtown Worcester for a department store—but he also scrutinized every item in fitting up the laboratories, on some occasions, it is claimed, insisting upon his own judgment in opposition to that of the faculty member concerned.

On the other hand, there is considerable evidence that finances and administrative problems connected with them were by no means the only source of difficulty. In any such situation as that at Clark personal relationships loom large. President Hall had done a remarkable job in selecting men for the new institution, and had made possible for the faculty conditions with respect to freedom of teaching and research that were recognized as almost ideal. He had, however, been rather less successful in establishing and maintaining satisfactory personal relations with some of the men whom he had brought to Worcester. Dissatisfaction developed among the faculty

---

[15] G. Stanley Hall, *Life and Confessions of a Psychologist*, p. 291.

and came to a head in the middle of the third year. On January 21, 1892, a majority of the members of the teaching staff, after a series of meetings at the homes of one of the group, signed a communication to the board of trustees resigning their positions on the ground that they had "lost confidence" in President Hall. In his autobiographical account Hall attributes this action to lack of understanding by the staff of the peculiar financial situation and the inability of the president and the board to tell the whole story for fear of alienating Mr. Clark. Whatever the actual conditions, some members of the faculty, as indicated in the "lost-confidence" letter, did not trust Dr. Hall. They felt, to use Hall's own words, that he had "deceived them." Undoubtedly a group made up of as striking and diverse personalities as Hall had brought together would be difficult to manage. "We do not need to assume any more than average human frailty," says Dr. Amy Tanner, author of an unpublished history of the early days of Clark—and accusations of unfairness or worse where a president is concerned are not uncommon in the best university circles—but it is significant that serious dissension had apparently developed prior to a time when the financial pinch could have been known or felt. Moreover, there can be little question that these faculty doubts as to some aspects of President Hall's administration reached Mr. Clark and influenced his attitude toward the future of the institution. Mr. Clark, himself, says Dr. Tanner, "was not a genial man, and was keenly conscious of his lack of formal education. He could not find much common ground on which to meet either his trustees or faculty, and so when misunderstandings rose, explanations were difficult and unsatisfactory, and his tendency was to revert to the attitude of an employer to a hired hand." [16]

Real Difference in Point of View

Fundamentally, however, there was a real difference in point of view between Clark and Hall as to what the University ought to do. "We must bear in mind," says Louis Wilson, "that Mr. Clark from the very first intended to found a college for undergraduates, and that he held tenaciously to this idea to the very last."

Mr. Clark had always desired a college for men after the New England type. Dr. Hall persuaded him to try first, for three years, a purely graduate institution. Each probably hoped to win the other over to his views before the three years came to an end. But instead of drawing nearer to each

[16] Letter of September 4, 1938. Dr. Tanner adds: "It is rather pathetic that when the Doctors' theses began to be printed, he always had some on the table in his 'front parlor' where callers could easily see them—the only tangible return for his money."

other, they drifted apart; and when a number of the Faculty became rest-
less . . . Dr. Hall let them go without informing them how meager the endowment was, and Mr. Clark probably saw them go with a certain sense
of satisfaction in the hope that he might at last be able to carry out his
original idea of a college for boys.

Wilson questions, it should be noted, whether Clark really ever accepted
or understood Hall's conception of a university devoted to research, even
though the trustees, with one possible exception, seem to have supported
Hall's views. "It is hardly fair to criticize our Founder because he failed to
found such an institution as Dr. Hall had in mind," says Wilson. "He had
contemplated for a great many years an institution of a particular kind, and
at his age it was almost impossible for him to cast aside his own child and
adopt another's." And he points out that Dr. Hall's conception of a university devoted solely to research, while it would have been "the outstanding
feature in American education in this generation, had it been possible to
carry it out," was still an unattained goal at the time he wrote (1927):

In the twenty-seven years that have elapsed since Mr. Clark's death
enormous sums of money have been given to higher education by wealthy
men, but such an institution as Dr. Hall contemplated has not yet been
founded. Evidently Mr. Clark was not the only large donor who has
failed to appreciate this wonderful idea.[17]

On the other hand, Mr. Clark's ideas were hardly limited to the collegiate
plan he finally insisted upon in his will as the "principal feature" of the
University. In his address at the opening exercises of the University in 1889
the founder had specified that one of the objectives was to be "scientific
research and investigation," and in his will he described his original plan
as designed to establish an institution which should "combine in effective
cooperation" three departments—one "for original research in the acqui-
sition of knowledge," a second "for general and liberal instruction to students
and attendance," and a third, the library, "which might, to some extent,
under proper restrictions, be opened for general use." Calvin Stebbins has
testified that "Mr. Clark's ideal of a university was large and ample, yes,
truly magnificent." Every department of human learning was contemplated
in Mr. Clark's thinking, Dr. Stebbins asserts, but he was convinced that
Mr. Clark had an inadequate idea of the cost of such an enterprise, that
he recalled the meager beginnings of Harvard and other established seats
of learning, that he believed educational institutions should grow rather

---

[17] Louis N. Wilson, "Some Recollections of Our Founder," p. 8.

than merely expand, that he felt the large endowment he had provided should have gone further than it did. Moreover, Mr. Clark felt keenly the handicaps poor boys had who lacked college training, as he did; he was particularly interested in country boys, sincerely believing that they had a significant part to play in American business and commercial life because of their early farm training in hard work; and he wished to make sure that the educational interests of these youngsters from the rural sections were steadfastly kept in mind.[18] President Hall's insistence upon the highly specialized graduate function of Clark University made the founder more and more sceptical of him, more and more fearful lest the original objective would be lost sight of in anything that Hall would have to deal with—hence the provision in the Clark will whereby Dr. Hall was not to head the undergraduate college set up under it. It is quite likely, as Wilson points out, that the two men realized that they were not really in agreement, even at the beginning, but that each felt he might eventually be able to modify the position of the other sufficiently to get what he felt was necessary. President Hall was always trying ways of getting the founder more definitely on record in favor of the graduate university research idea. He missed no opportunity to have Mr. Clark join in taking the responsibility for the kind of university Hall visioned. Of course, it became more and more difficult, with Hall less and less successfully pushing and Clark more and more silently resistant, gradually withdrawing not only his support but his presence at board meetings and his contact with board members. In its less tragic aspects it became a sort of game. As one of the most distinguished of the original Clark faculty described it years afterward,[19] Mr. Clark would drive out from town in his carriage to the University; President Hall would use his extraordinary powers of persuasion and seemingly get Mr. Clark committed to a particular course of action involving expenditure of some of Mr. Clark's money; Mr. Clark would depart, and then would ensue something of a scramble to get the plan into action before Mr. Clark could change his mind.

In any case, it was a real crisis that confronted Clark University in this third year, both financially and educationally. The decline in income resulting from Mr. Clark's withdrawal meant drastic salary cuts or dismissals or both. A majority of the faculty were, for one reason or another, dissatisfied and ready to resign.

---

[18] Calvin Stebbins, "Address at Founder's Day Exercises," February 1, 1905. *Publications of the Clark University Library*, vol. 1, no. 6, April, 1905, p. 158.

[19] Henry H. Donaldson in an interview at the Wistar Institute, Philadelphia, November 22, 1937.

President Harper's Visit to Clark

It was at this juncture that President William Rainey Harper of the University of Chicago appeared on the scene. He was having difficulty in securing an adequate staff for his new University. He had been apprised of the faculty discontent at Worcester, and had been told that he could probably get there some of the men he needed most, in biology and other fields. Survivors of the early Clark days are clear in their recollections, already cited, that the financial motive was not the sole or even the most impelling one. Many of the staff, it is understood, would have been glad to stay under any reasonable arrangements that could have been made, but felt they must leave because of the dissatisfaction with President Hall's attitude toward them indicated in the communication of January, 1892, to the board and freely admitted in Hall's own account. A group did stay, of course: William H. Burnham, Alexander F. Chamberlain, Clifton F. Hodge, Edmund C. Sanford, William E. Story, Henry Taber, Arthur G. Webster.

Even after the lapse of years, when Hall came to write in the autobiography of the Harper visit, he was so emotionally stirred that one feels obligated to omit whole sentences here and there from the account in the interest of historical perspective and calm. In brief, he stated that "Dr. Harper, learning of the dissatisfaction here, had at Professor Whitman's house met and engaged one morning the majority of our staff . . . taking even instructors, docents, and fellows. . . . When this was done he called on me, inviting me also to join the hegira, which of course I refused. . . . I replied that it was an act of wreckage for us. . . . I finally told him that if he would revise the list, releasing a few of our men and taking one or two others whom he had omitted, I would bear the calamity silently and with what grace I could."[20]

It is impossible to say, of course, to what extent Dr. Hall might have regained control of the situation if the men who were dissatisfied had not had this "unparalleled offer" from President Harper at just this time. Dr. Tanner remarks:

> I think we may be rather sure that even if they had been on the best possible terms with Dr. Hall and the Board few of them could have refused the opportunity to go into new laboratories, in beautiful buildings fitted with every possible convenience, with much more to spend for equipment, books, laboratory assistants, etc.; with the background of a big city containing rare libraries, medical schools and other facilities that Clark could

[20] G. Stanley Hall, *Life and Confessions of a Psychologist*, p. 296.

never duplicate, and with no Founder dropping in every day or so. After all, they had only been at Clark three years, not long enough to get the corners rubbed off so they could roll around comfortably together, and not long enough to develop a distinctive Clark spirit.[21]

Three of the Clark men went immediately to head the departments of chemistry, physics, and biology at the University of Chicago—departments doing graduate work, as it happened, made possible by the Ogden Fund, of which Andrew H. Green, a native of Worcester, was trustee. Of sixteen biologists at Clark in 1891–92, all but four went to Chicago.[22] "Thus," says Hall in the autobiography, "Clark had served as a nursery, for most of our faculty were simply transplanted to a richer financial soil."

President Harper, Professor Sanford remarks, "endorsed the quality of Dr. Hall's selections at the same time that he took from him men who would be sorely missed." Others of the staff found university posts elsewhere— Warren P. Lombard at Michigan, for example—and by the close of the academic year only two men of full faculty rank remained.[23] "Both the trustees and I would have withdrawn could we have done so honorably," wrote President Hall years afterward, "but this seemed impossible. So we heartened each other as best we could and went on through the seven long moratorium years of watchful waiting, which were overhung by the great and all-pervading fear that the founder would bestow elsewhere the residue of his fortune, of the size of which we knew nothing."[24]

AFTER THE HEGIRA

Clark University had never been large, but it opened its fourth year in September, 1892 with about half the faculty and enrollment it had had the year before—a total of twelve members of the instructional staff and forty students. Those who stayed, however, were, from all the evidence available, enthusiastic and able. It was anything but a failure. Indeed, President Hall's account in the autobiography reveals clearly his own surprise at the way those who remained carried on:

We closed up the ranks as best we could and settled down in a spirit of exceptional harmony and close fellowship to make the most and best we

[21] Letter of September 4, 1938.

[22] As shown in a contemporary photograph in the possession of Professor Frank R. Lillie, 1938.

[23] Edmund C. Sanford, "A Sketch of the History of Clark University," *Publications of the Clark University Library*, vol. 7, no. 1, January, 1923, p. 3.

[24] G. Stanley Hall, *Life and Confessions of a Psychologist*, p. 6.

could of the only income, namely $24,000 a year plus that of the library, that we had until Mr. Clark's death. . . .

It was nothing less than amazing to me to see how the little group of young, often very young, men who studied and especially those who taught here, grew intellectually as if by leaps and bounds. In our small sphere we certainly had a seminarium which in both its soil and atmosphere stimulated all to grow at a state in their development when academic practices had so generally been averse to their advancement.[25]

Every member of the staff of 1892 stuck to his post, in spite of offers to go elsewhere, for the next twenty-one years.[26] Hall himself re-entered the classroom, making a contribution regarded by competent observers as so significant that it must necessarily be discussed hereafter in analyzing the factors that entered into the Clark achievement. Faculty organization was simplified. The original limitation to five departments was even more rigorously adhered to, and chemistry was soon dropped. The President's Report of 1893 stated that "Clark University is exclusively what is called in Europe a Philosophical Faculty, or a part of one so far as yet developed, devoted to a group of the *pure sciences* which underlie technology and medicine, but not yet applying its work to these professional fields." Actually, however, the chief resources of the University were now no longer in the pure sciences to the extent they were before, but in psychology and education, where Hall's own abilities had, of course, the largest scope.

The Two Clark Periods

There were thus two periods in the early history of Clark: a brilliant first three years in which biology and other physical sciences were conspicuous, and a second period, dominated to a large extent by Dr. Hall himself, in which psychology and education played the major role.

Professor Sanford insists, in his historical sketch of 1923, that the original ideals of Clark University were well maintained in the years following the 1892 reorganization, "though upon a much smaller scale than had originally been hoped."[27] He sees the story as "the uneventful chronicle of students trained, scientific journals edited, researches made and books written and published." Toward the end of this period enough had been accomplished to warrant a modest celebration of the completion of a decade of university work, and the standing of the institution was still such that a group of

[25] Ibid., pp. 297–298; 303.

[26] Louis N. Wilson, "Biographical Sketch," p. 30.

[27] Edmund C. Sanford, "A Sketch of the History of Clark University," p. 5.

European scholars of first rank came to participate. Indeed, it remained one of Dr. Hall's "sources of mortification" that, as a result of his European trip in 1889 and the persistent sympathy with what was being attempted at Worcester, there was among European scholars an "uncritical assumption that Clark University, which in fact proved to be a very small institution, was a leader if not the capstone of the entire American educational system."[28]

Hall himself insisted throughout that "the only distinction we clung to was that we took only graduates and devoted ourselves to research. That was the chief unique feature we could plead." The rather moderate statement prefaced to the account of the decennial celebration says:

Clark University has confined itself to truly postgraduate work in a few departments, and has admitted such students only as gave promise of the ability not only to pursue the courses here offered with advantage to themselves, but to benefit the world by advancing science along the lines here represented. It has thus taken a distinct position as a training school for college professors and scientific investigators. Such a policy is conducive neither to large numbers of students nor to popular appreciation. But, small as the university is and few as are its departments, it takes great satisfaction in pointing to this volume as, in some sense, a record of its work and its methods. The list of titles of the publications of its past and present members is a witness of the quality and quantity of what it has accomplished. We believe that Clark University, opening, as it did, at the beginning of a new university epoch in this country, has had some special influence in suggesting new lines of scientific research.[29]

Some distinguished educational leaders of the day were more outspoken than the officers of Clark in estimating what the University had been able to accomplish in these ten years. President W. H. P. Faunce of Brown University felt it safe to say that "Clark University has done more to widen the confines of human knowledge than any other American college in one hundred and fifty years." United States Commissioner of Education William T. Harris labeled this first decade of Clark as "one of the most wonderful careers to be chronicled in the history of American education" and said the Clark movement was all the more valuable because it challenged the aims and purposes of the present existing education. One of the most interesting comments at the decennial came from a man who had a very special reason for understanding the significance of the work at Worcester—Frederic Burk, a Clark man himself, at that time head of the San Francisco State

[28] G. Stanley Hall, *Life and Confessions of a Psychologist*, p. 279.
[29] *Clark University, 1889–1899: Decennial Celebration*, p. iii.

Normal School, and an educational innovator whose pioneering efforts have begun to be understood and appreciated only in comparatively recent times. Burk wrote:

No undertaking nor movement has made so clear and definite impress upon the educational thought of America nor established guiding lines of control so distinctly in pedagogical and psychological progress as the suggestions and tendencies which have emanated from Clark University. Though the institution is yet in its infancy, though the students in point of numbers have been limited, yet its influence has penetrated every state in the Union, has entered practically every educational institution of the land, from university to kindergarten, and has quickened the spirit of educational conferences, from those of national repute to those of the little teachers' meetings of the village school.

Granting the truth of the educational view for which Clark University stands, and allowing for the singularly forceful methods of instruction by the President and Faculty within the institution, and the energy with which its mission has been prosecuted, it is nevertheless still a marvel that its influence should have become, in this brief space, so widespread and vigorous. The facts which stand prove the wisdom of the plan of an institution which should be exclusively graduate, selecting as its students a limited number of mature thinkers who should be inspired by the power which ever comes from the contact with original investigation and a faculty of original investigators.[30]

When Jonas Clark died in 1900 it was found that he had carried out his plan of providing for an undergraduate department. He specified that Hall should not head this institution, but that it was to be set up independently, though using the same library, grounds, and buildings as the already existent University. The will provided considerable addition to the independent endowment of the University Library, established a University art gallery, and made a small addition to the funds of Clark University itself.

The Accomplishments of Twelve Years

A University statement prepared in 1901 undertook to tell briefly what had been accomplished in twelve years in the effort to do in a very few departments "the most costly as well as the highest of all scientific educational work":

[Clark University] has given the country a new type of institution, with no college or undergraduate department, and hence no classes, dormi-

---

[30] Ibid., p. 34.

tories, discipline, or commencements, where the chief effort of its faculties in their collective capacities has been to solve the new and higher university problems in some of which it has led the way and contributed to bring back the apex of our American system of education from Europe, where hundreds of our best graduates formerly had to go to finish their training, to our own country. As the only purely postgraduate institution in the country, it has thus stood for a new and higher ideal, helped to make it practicable, and was the first upon this higher plane.

It has fitted for this work 386 young men who are now mostly professors or instructors in colleges and normal schools, and nearly every one of those who have studied here is engaged in higher education. Clark men have won positions in the faculties or teaching staffs of Harvard, Yale, Johns Hopkins, Columbia, Chicago, Stanford, California, Toronto, Michigan, and in scores of other institutions in nearly every State in the Union.

In the years that followed the increase in endowment received under Mr. Clark's will made possible somewhat more adequate faculty salaries and a slight expansion of facilities. The Chemistry Department was reopened; the Department of Psychology was strengthened; beginnings were eventually made in the Departments of History and Social Science. The second decennial of the University was celebrated in 1909 with a conference similar to that of 1899, this time also with the help of a visiting group of outstanding men in science from Europe and representatives from colleges, universities, and technical schools in the United States. Dr. Hall's twenty-fifth anniversary as president was commemorated in 1914, and in 1920 Dr. Hall withdrew from the responsibilities he had held for thirty-two years.

The present study does not attempt to deal with recent developments at Clark. It is worth noting, however, that in selecting a few fields of learning and doing intensive work with selected students under highly competent direction the University is again following the principle on which its early successes in part at least depended.

ELEMENTS IN THE CLARK ACHIEVEMENT

In the last years of his life President G. Stanley Hall wrote that "small as Clark was, and whatever its importance, in its plan and in its story it was unique."

Although the Clark University experiment was not permitted by circumstances to develop with the fullness that had been planned and suffered an almost irreparable blow very early in its career, it had an influence upon university education, particularly at the graduate level, far beyond anything that its finances and numbers would suggest. Particularly noteworthy is it that its successes went on without being affected to anything like the extent one would expect them to have been by the disaster of 1892. Were the elements in the Clark story such that one must regard it as unique, as Dr. Hall partly implies in the sentence just quoted from him, or were they, in part at least, elements that are possible for any sincere graduate enterprise, and may well be employed where the resources are the simplest and the grandiose is neither required nor desired? With full recognition of the fact that a new enterprise by the very fact that it is new often captures the imagination and leads commonplace men to achieve uncommonly well, and with clear realization of the rather special uniqueness of some of the personalities involved, especially that of G. Stanley Hall himself, were there factors in the Clark University experience that are just as valid today as they were in the 'eighties and 'nineties and therefore worth looking into for the sake of graduate education today and in the future?

MEETING GENUINE NEEDS

As with Johns Hopkins, there was first of all in the Clark situation a resolute determination to meet what were felt to be urgent contemporary needs that were not being met in the higher institutions of the day. Andrew D. White, always thinking positively of what university training might mean in the United States, urged upon Hall the necessity of developing in the new University "the highest study and research" in such fields as science, and recommended particularly that the emphasis be placed upon selection and quality:

> If you will send out each year twenty, or ten, or even five men fitted to take leading places as professors, teachers, experts, leaders in public discussions, in the press and elsewhere, on important subjects, you will, I fully believe, do a greater work than you can do in any other way.

Wolcott Gibbs wanted the new enterprise to be devoted almost exclusively to the work of scientific research—using the word scientific in its highest and not in any narrow sense. At present, he said, "there is no university which covers this ground."[31] These and other advisers were pointing out, just as they had when Gilman was organizing the Hopkins, that advanced work of genuine university quality in contrast to a narrow collegiate program of studies was urgently needed in America. President Barnard of Columbia had commented in his report for 1870 that "the colleges, in insisting upon

---

[31] *Early Proceedings of the Board of Trustees of Clark University*, Worcester, Massachusetts, 1901.

the pursuance of an invariable curriculum of study by all their students, are not satisfying the demand of the age as it respects the higher education," and he explained the increased enrollments at Harvard at a time when other New England colleges were losing students as due to the fact that "Harvard has been progressively more and more completely identifying herself with the cause of the new education, and more and more liberally enlarging her facilities to give it." [32] Nicholas Murray Butler, commenting at a somewhat later date on the status of higher education, pointed out that "with the exception of Johns Hopkins and Clark University every existing American university is the outgrowth of an earlier and older college, and for both of these an organization for undergraduate work was quickly provided." [33]

In Behalf of Science

Partly because of this history behind them, it was notably difficult to get American colleges and universities to recognize the needs for an education— Eliot, Gilman, and others of their day called it the "new education"—in which science and scientific research would be adequately recognized. This was one of the needs Clark University tried to meet. In his address at the Clark opening, October 22, 1889, Senator George F. Hoar, President of the Board of Trustees, found it necessary to defend science in fairly strong words:

Speaking now for myself alone, I have little sympathy with that arrogant and disdainful spirit with which some men who undertake, with little title, to represent science in this country, sneer at any attempt to make use of the forces she reveals to us for the service of mankind. Some one said the other day, that science was becoming a hod-carrier. I do not see why the term "hod-carrier" should express the relation rather than the term "benefactress." I do not see, either, that there is anything degrading in the thought that the knowledge of the learned man enables him to lift the burden, beneath which humanity is bowed and bent. I do not know that science is exempt from the divine law, "He that is greatest among you, let him be the servant of all." If the great forces of the universe perform all useful offices for man, if the sunshine warm and light our dwellings, if gravitation move the world and keep it true to its hour, nay, if it keep the temple or cathedral in its place when the hod-carrier has builded it, I do not see why it should not lend its beneficent aid to him also. Our illustrious philosopher advised his countryman to "hitch his wagon to a star." The star will move no less serenely on its sublime pathway when the wagon

---

[32] *The Rise of a University*, New York, Columbia University Press, 1937, vol. I, pp. 91–92.
[33] Ibid., vol. II, p. 369.

is hitched to it. I do not know that any archangel or goddess, however re-splendent the wings, has yet been constructed or imagined without feet. I do not know that any archangel, however glorious, has ever been created or imagined without sympathy for suffering humanity.

I look for great advantage to the country, both in wealth and power and in the comfort and moral improvement of the people by the application of science to the useful arts.[34]

At Clark, as at Hopkins, the purpose was to meet what were conceived to be the needs of the day, rather than merely to follow a college and university tradition. Simple as this principle is, it is probably the most difficult to invoke consistently and the easiest to forget. It involves constantly re-facing the educational task in the light of the changes in human society. Of course there is always something a little uncomfortable about this; it presupposes a restlessness and willingness to change that become less and less character-istic of people and institutions after a time. No human enterprises are im-mune; the daring adventurer of yesterday becomes the stereotype of today, still talking as if he were blazing trails; and institutions are even more so. At Clark University Hall's leadership, whatever else may be said of it, was so dynamic and his connection with the social and educational stirring of his time so lively and intimate that much of the freshness of the first days survived beyond the customary period of institutional youthfulness. And those who went forth from Clark to educational enterprises of their own were quite likely to be known for their adherence to this principle and its appli-cation to their own situations—an excellent indication of its soundness and the effective way in which it must have been learned at Clark.

MEN OR BUILDINGS?

In one sense Clark University was not so fortunate as the Johns Hopkins: whereas Gilman was not permitted under the terms of his grant to erect buildings out of capital funds, but was obliged to put his resources into men —both faculty and students—the founder of Clark University was literally out working for many months to get a building erected so that a university might begin! Stanley Hall himself, however, was perfectly clear on this point. He liked good educational buildings, and he was especially partial to ingen-ious laboratory equipment (though he preferred that wherever possible it be built on the premises), but his eyes were set on people—on the best pos-sible people he could secure to direct instruction and research. It is this that

[34] *Early Proceedings of the Board of Trustees of Clark University*, Worcester, Massachusetts, 1901.

made the faculty losses of 1892 so tragic for Hall. "We had brought together," he says in the autobiography, "a teaching force in these departments then nowhere equalled in the country. . . . I had been allowed absolute freedom in the selection of men, and in this matter no suggestion ever came either from Mr. Clark or any member of his board." Again: "I had spent much time, travel, and effort in gathering this very distinguished group of men, and I told him [Dr. Harper] that his action was like that of the eagle who robbed the fishhawk of his prey."[35] Nearly a half century later one of the original Worcester group who was often critical of Hall paid tribute to the president on this score: "Hall had a fine ideal," he said, "and selected an excellent group of men. . . . The answer to the question as to the success of Hopkins, Clark, and Chicago, is: *men of ability, professors and students, with sufficient funds to carry on their work, time for research, and freedom to work in their own way.* Buildings are a nuisance if they require too much housekeeping. One ought to be able to drive a nail wherever it is needed."[36]

It is significant that almost the only mention of building activities in Clark University official publications is at the very beginning, when Jonas Clark is depicted busily supervising the erection of what is still one of the main university structures. Thereafter it is the names of individual faculty members, instructors, docents, and others that are featured—long lists of them, as in the third annual report (1893), where the list in psychology, for example, is interesting not only because of the detail into which it goes, but because a fairly large proportion of the names will be recognized as of men who achieved distinction in their chosen fields:

The Department of Psychology, headed at first by President Hall himself, included anthropology, neurology, and education. Members, 1889–1893— G. Stanley Hall; Henry H. Donaldson, assistant professor of neurology; Clifton F. Hodge, fellow and assistant in neurology; Edmund C. Sanford, instructor in psychology; William H. Burnham, docent in pedagogy, later instructor; A. F. Chamberlain, fellow in anthropology, later lecturer in anthropology; Benjamin Ives Gilman, instructor in psychology; Franz Boas, docent in anthropology; B. C. Burt, docent in philosophy; Alfred Cook, docent in philosophy; Arthur MacDonald, docent in ethics; Charles H. Strong, docent in philosophy; H. Austin Aikins, fellow in psychology; Ernest Albee, scholar, later fellow in psychology; Thomas P. Bailey, Jr.,

---

[35] It should be noted, however, that Hall had already lost these men before Harper came. See pp. 58 f.

[36] Letter of Dr. Warren P. Lombard, University of Michigan, Ann Arbor, Michigan, May 17, 1938. Dr. Lombard's words suggest those that a colleague of his, Professor William H. Burnham, made into a series of principles applicable to all education—"a task, a plan, and freedom." (See *The Normal Mind*, New York, D. Appleton-Century Company, 1925.)

fellow in psychology; J. A. Bergström, fellow in psychology; Thaddeus L. Bolton, scholar, later fellow and assistant in psychology; William L. Bryan, fellow in psychology; Oscar Chrisman, fellow in pedagogy; Arthur H. Daniels, fellow in psychology; F. B. Dresslar, scholar, later fellow in psychology; Alexander Fraser, fellow in psychology; Daniel Fulcomer, fellow in psychology; E. A. Kirkpatrick, scholar, later fellow in psychology; William O. Krohn, fellow in psychology; James E. LeRossignol, fellow in psychology; Dickinson S. Miller, fellow in psychology; Herbert Nichols, fellow in psychology; E. W. Scripture, fellow in psychology; Frederick Tracy, fellow in psychology; Gerald M. West, fellow in anthropology; Walter Channing, honorary scholar, later honorary fellow; E. N. Brown, scholar in psychology; Frank Drew, scholar in psychology; John P. Fruit, scholar in psychology; R. C. Hollenbaugh, scholar in psychology; James H. Leuba, scholar, later fellow in psychology; C. A. Orr, scholar in psychology; Jefferson R. Potter, scholar in psychology; J. F. Reigart, scholar in psychology; Toshihide Shinoda, James S. Lemon, Arvin S. Olin, Edward W. Flagg, Jinzo Naruse.

METHODS OF INSTRUCTION

Above the entrance to the School of Geography workroom at the Clark University of today are inscribed Charles William Eliot's words: *The very best kind of education is obtained in doing things one's self under competent direction and with good guidance.*

The type of teaching and learning relationship implied in President Eliot's statement was especially evident at Clark. As with the Johns Hopkins, informality prevailed in the relations between faculty and students, made possible quite as much by the attitude toward scholarship and research as by the small number of students. President Hall himself led the way. A recently retired university dean who was at Clark in the early days[37] says that Hall was one of the most generous men he ever knew from the point of view of "sharing scholarship"; that students who came to Clark from other universities where it was the recognized practice for the head of the department to publish the work of his students as "by Professor——, assisted by [names of students]," were amazed to find that at Clark Dr. Hall encouraged the graduate student to publish the material under the student's own name and seldom claimed any of the credit.[38] When Dr. George E. Dawson, at a gathering of Clark alumni in 1907, was enumerating the fea-

[37] Frederick E. Bolton, of the University of Washington, in an interview at Seattle, July 13, 1938.

[38] Dr. Warren P. Lombard notes that Hall had had an excellent example set him in this respect in Ludwig's laboratories at Leipzig. (Interview of August 21, 1938.)

tures of Clark University that might justifiably be regarded as "unique," he found himself listing a number of points all centering upon this human relationship at Clark: that every student was made to feel that he stood for something; that the teachers were greater as friends than they were as pedagogues ("and this is saying much, for greater teachers, each in his own way, I have not known"); that there was a "faith in men and a friendship for men."[39]

Faculty and Student Relations

The peculiar advantage of Clark University, said Frederick C. Ferry (then at Williams, later president of Hamilton College) at the time of the Decennial Celebration, "is mainly attributable to the close and personal relations between professors and students under which the work is conducted." Pointing out that the formal lecture delivered to a body of men in the class-room has but little of the stimulative force imparted by a conversational discussion with the man alone in the lecturer's private study, he said that too great praise could hardly be given to the faculty of Clark "for their constant and generous sacrifice of time to this most helpful method of instruction."[40] Professor G. H. Blakeslee in a recent unpublished paper quotes Hall as saying in substance to three young instructors upon their appointment to the graduate faculty: "When Clark started we were ten years ahead of other American universities, and when they had caught up to where we were, we were still ten years ahead. It is your privilege to help maintain this leadership." Chancellor Harry W. Chase says that what Hall seemed always to be trying to do was give his students a sense of the joy in research. "He tried to make us see, not drudgery and heavy routine, but the fascination and the glories of the search for truth."[41]

President Hall had stated the point of view clearly in his first annual report:

> For those students whom we receive we should do everything possible for instructors to do. They should be personally aided, guided to the best literature, and advanced by every method that pedagogic skill and sym-

[39] Proceedings at the first annual banquet of the New England Association of Alumni of Clark University and at the banquet of the Washington, D. C. Alumni Association, 1907. *Publications of the Clark University Library*, vol. 2, no. 4, June, 1907.

[40] *Clark University, 1889–1899: Decennial Celebration*, p. 36. President-emeritus Ferry has since told how he was invited to become a member of the staff at Clark, but declined. (Letter of October 19, 1938.)

[41] Harry W. Chase, "Granville Stanley Hall, February 1, 1844–April 24, 1924, In Memoriam," *Publications of the Clark University Library*, vol. 7, no. 6, May, 1925, p. 63.

pathy can devise. They should feel all the enthusiasm, understand all the interests, and all the methods of the instructor. He should confidentially share with them all his hopes and plans for research.

"The very attitude of research," he said later, "is more and more seen to be the best method of educating the maturer students in all fields, because it trains the power of effort, cultivates initiative, strengthens the will, and gives that individual independence of judgment and action in which modern culture culminates. . . . It gives teaching a new power and zest. Instruction to a fit few by an investigator who stands on the frontier and feels the heat and light which attends discovery is inspiring, and is very different from information imparted at lower levels by teachers further removed from the work of discovery and creation."[42]

Later educators, inspired in part by the child study movement for which Hall himself was furnishing leadership, were able to show that something of the same thrill of "discovery and creation" might be possible on other than the graduate level, and involved an important principle for all education, not simply graduate study. Moreover, Hall's use of the word "creation" indicates that he had a more dynamic notion of research than was to be found later on in some universities claiming to carry on the research tradition. Indeed, many a university graduate school was destined to have said of it with considerable justification what Hall said of certain institutions of his day:

> There is no institution that should be more respected than a university that is old and large, whether in Europe or America. . . . Yet age which brings wisdom may bring infirmities. . . . Saddest of all, perhaps, departments of endowed knowledge, like professors, sometimes cease to be productive and grow dry, formal, sterile. . . . In this country we need new men, new measures, and occasionally new universities.[43]

The freshness of point of view evidenced in the university pioneering at Clark made a deep impression on some of the best men of the time, who felt the need for more of a living force in higher education. Edward Everett Hale

---

[42] Clark University, second annual report, 1891.

[43] The conception of research was not always quickly grasped by the universities. In his biography of Eliot, Henry James quotes Professor C. L. Jackson as saying that "when he was a young teacher of chemistry in the 'seventies he asked Eliot if he might be relieved of the duty of teaching one class in order to prosecute certain investigations. The president, in his stately manner, proposed a question to which an answer can seldom be given: 'What will be the result of these investigations?' 'They would be published,' was the reply. The president wanted to know where. Mr. Jackson named a German chemical journal. 'I can't see that that will serve any useful purpose here,' said Eliot, and therewith dismissed the matter." (Henry James, *Charles William Eliot*, vol. II, p. 19.)

thought the experiment at Clark might mean that we were learning in America something more fundamental than we had known before about the whole matter of education at maturity levels:

The truth is America does not yet understand what the teaching of men is. . . . When we have a thoughtful, investigating man who has come to be two and twenty, has the fulness of his power, and is eager to keep up his studies, we turn him out of our college, and say, "We have nothing more for you." And when we have a man who is determined to devote his life for others, we thank him and say, "We will make you a professor in a college; we will give you fifteen hundred dollars a year, while with your ability you would earn fifteen thousand somewhere else." And then we set him to teaching boys of eighteen the difference between the subjunctive and the optative, or showing them the mistakes they have made in their German exercises where they have put in a masculine article instead of a feminine.[44]

"Receptivity" Versus "Creative Research"

The finer university spirit has seldom been more eloquently expressed than by President Hall at the Clark Decennial Celebration. The "well furnished bachelor of arts," said Hall, on turning from the "receptivity" type of knowledge to "creative research," is at first helpless, and needs personal direction and management before he can walk alone.

But when the new powers are once acquired they are veritable regeneration. He scorns the mere luxury of knowing, and wishes to achieve, to become an authority and not an echo. His ambition is to know how it looks near and beyond the frontier of knowledge, and to wrest if possible a new inch of territory from the nascent realm of chaos and old night, and this becomes a new and consuming passion which makes him feel a certain kinship with the creative minds of all ages, and having contributed ever so little, he realizes for the first time what true intellectual freedom is, and attains intellectual manhood and maturity. This thrill of discovery, once felt, is the royal accolade of science, which says to the novice, "stand erect, look about you, that henceforth you may light your own way with independent knowledge."

This higher educational realm is full of new "phenomena of altitude," said Hall, and wherever it is established "faculties, instead of discussing and elaborating plans for commencement ceremonies, hearing recitations, pre-

[44] Edward Everett Hale, "Clark University," in "Tarry at Home Travels—1889," *New England Magazine*, 39:243–246, October, 1908.

paring and then reading the results of examination papers, and carefully marking each individual exercise, grinding in the old mills of parietal regulations, discipline, and the rules of conduct needful to civilize the adolescent *homo sapiens ferus*, revising requirements for admission, tacking and shaping the policy to gather in more students and keep ahead of others in the struggle to get the best connections with high and fitting schools, are occupied with far different problems." They find that they must discriminate abilities, learn to detect early manifestations of talent and genius, and having done this, to help the university bestow freely its needed aid and equipment and the professor his choicest time and knowledge, to perfect the precious environment:

Having thus sown fit seed in fit soil, it must be watched and watered with constant suggestion. The best and newest literature; the most effective and original apparatus that can be devised and if possible made on the spot; how to insure in the best form and place the speedy publication of work and to bring it under the eye of all experts; how to avoid conflict and duplication; how general or how special thesis subjects and work should be to best combine the two sometimes more or less divergent ends of discovery and education; the requirements for perhaps the choicest of all degrees, the doctorate of philosophy; the best modes of individual examination for it; the number and relation of subjects required; the migration of students so as to insure not only the best environment for each, but to give to professors not only in the same department, but in different institutions, the same stimulus that was felt when the elective system aroused the dry-as-dust professors to unwonted effort lest their classrooms be left vacant; the kindred question of the relative value of graduate work at home and abroad for each student and for each department; the great problem of printing and special journals together with interchange of monographs; the vast new library problems of purveying for highly specialized, but very voracious, appetites which make the true university librarian a man of far different order from others, and gives him a wealth of new problems of exchange, foraging, etc., to maintain the true relations between lecture work and individual guidance while duly emancipating the professors from the drudgery of elementary teaching and mass treatment of great bodies of students; the many and wide-reaching differences between pure and applied science, and the practical methods by which this distinction is maintained; the danger of great aggregations of students and the advantages of few; the wide differences between the new kind of professor needed in the university and those in the college, where no provision is made for the advancement of learning, and the tests are mainly pedagogic; the even greater contrasts between scholarship funds for the aid of poverty to professional careers, which are a doubtful advantage even in colleges where they belong, and the true university fellowship as above described; the growing dominance and need of expertness in all fields for which graduate departments must prepare as well as for professorships alone,—these and many great questions like them constitute the opening field of what may be called the higher educational statesmanship.[45]

THE "SEMINARY"

Routine college teaching would hardly fit into the Clark scheme of things as here conceived, nor could it account for the results achieved. "Stated lectures . . . are the smallest part," President Hall noted in one of his early reports:

Elbow-teaching is given in the laboratory, and there is individual and constant guidance of reading, as well as experimentation, if needed or desired. Clubs, conferences, and seminaries are held, where all important literature in a wide field, and in different languages, is read, each man taking a subject, and reading and reporting for the benefit of the others. Not only the information, but the insigh⁺, criticism, methods, and standpoint of each are pooled for the edification and stimulation of all. The contact between professor and student was never closer, and more avenues were never opened between minds working in the same place and field.

But it was the "Seminary," or *Seminar*, that was outstanding in the Clark procedure and still stirs the memories of Clark men who were there in Hall's day. "Dr. Hall's seminar was the most interesting educational experience I ever had," says Professor Lewis M. Terman, of Stanford University. Clark men everywhere "like to live again through the evening seminars, where all were treated as equals," Professor G. H. Blakeslee recalls—the papers, the discussions, "then the masterly summing up by Hall." "Hall was magnificent in his seminars," says President Bryan, "coming in with his arms loaded with books and lecturing in inspired fashion. Colleagues who disliked him nevertheless came to his lectures because they could not afford to miss what he said."

Hall had developed the seminary out of his experience in German universities and at Johns Hopkins. It can best be understood by reading his own description of it in the autobiography:

At Clark, for nearly thirty years, I have met my students at my house every Monday night from seven, often to eleven, occasionally till twelve

---

[45] *Clark University, 1889–1899: Decennial Celebration*, pp. 55–56.

and even later. In the early days, when the institution was small, we sometimes read, the leader of the evening epitomizing, Kant's *Critique*, Jowett's *Plato*, Schopenhauer, once (but not very successfully) attacking Wallace's Hegel, Darwin, Spencer, and going into the originals with Locke, Descartes, Spinoza, Hume, and others, and also reading Nietzsche and Bergson. But as the seminary grew, nearly all our time was devoted to the reading of generally two papers an evening, each student taking his turn (the sessions separated by a fifteen-minute recess for ventilation and light refreshments) with distinguished men brought in from outside several times a year for our edification.

No one was *ever required or urged to attend* so that the numbers fluctuated according to the interest in the man or the subject presented—itself a wholesome stimulus. From perhaps a dozen to seventy-five or more would be present, and as outsiders were allowed to come in only by invitation of a member, the gathering was given only a slightly esoteric character. Each regular member was expected to take his turn, once at least, for half a session during the year, and one of the older members, under my direction, arranged the program each week for the next. Educational topics were often presented in this way, although psychology had the leading place, and I deemed it advisable to give to the discussions and even to the topics presented the widest possible range. It would be interesting to look over, had it only been preserved, the list of themes actually before us, some seventy a year, but even from these the debates often ranged very widely. After each presentation, which was almost always written and must never exceed an hour, the discussion was open to all, and after perhaps a slight initial embarrassment during the first weeks of each year there was always the most active participation. I stood always ready myself to fill any gap on the program, and almost everything I have ever presented either here or in lecture has been freely and sometimes even bitterly challenged, so that I have often had to defend my own pet views against very able, as well as indifferent adversaries. Thus this has been a real and great stimulus to me personally. I have often afterward made notes of "apperçus" that came to me in these discussions or of facts and ideas presented by my students, to whom I am much indebted.

The seminary has been a workshop for theses, most of which have been read here, perhaps in sections, and thus the candidates for degrees have been able to draw upon the sources of information possessed by all other members so that it has been a pooling institution. Among these candidates there have been Protestants, Catholics, Jews, Armenians, Chinese, Japanese, Germans, Frenchmen, Englishmen, Negroes, and representatives of nearly every other nationality. There have been ultra-doctrinaires for anarchism, extreme socialists, Mormons, believers in telepathy, materialists, idealists, and spiritualists. Several times there have been discussions between Negroes and students from the south and there has been every shade of religious opinion from the extreme of devotion to a no less extreme of pantheism, skepticism, and materialism of every kind and degree. Of course these discussions have often become more or less bitter and personal but I have always insisted that every one had a right to his "say" and I believe that this method has, on the whole, tended to moderate ultra and doctrinaire views, while it has had the most liberalizing influence upon conservatives to have their most cherished opinions flouted and to be challenged to stand forth and give a reason for the faith that is in them. The core of all these discussions has, of course, been philosophical and more specifically psychological, but as scores of former members have written or told me that, on the whole, they derived more good from the seminary than from all else, I am convinced that the largest latitude has been abundantly justified. A great many of the discussions were educational, ranging all the way from the care of babies and even prenatal regimen to the work of universities and learned societies, and in this domain, too, I think the method has enriched the mental soil and brought lucidity.[46]

Discussing the value of the *Seminary* a quarter of a century after its inauguration at Clark, Dr. Amy Tanner found that two things especially stood out. First was the general survey which the various theses gave to students who were working in the field of child psychology, keeping them, Miss Tanner said, "in touch with numerous lines of work that we should not be able to follow in our individual reading." But far more important, she maintained, was the opportunity to watch Dr. Hall's skill in leading a man to do a piece of work that was not only worth while to him but of value to others. Of course it was inevitable under any such plan that poor papers should be read sometimes, she went on, but "still it is true that in their preparation many men for the first time do independent work and feel a delight of constructive thinking." Not only this, but "as a rule the subject is so adapted to the man as to call out his best work and develop his highest interests, so that even though he be crude and ill-informed, in general he attains the front rank." Addressing Dr. Hall directly Miss Tanner concluded:

To discover these higher possibilities and powers is a task requiring the greatest pedagogical skill and one in which you are adept. It is in itself of the highest educative value to watch you in the Seminary, sometimes

---

[46] G. Stanley Hall, *Life and Confessions of a Psychologist*, pp. 326–329. An earlier account (written at the end of the first eight years) is given in Louis N. Wilson's *G. Stanley Hall: a Sketch*, New York, G. E. Stechert, 1914, pp. 101–103.

building up the confidence of the youth in himself and his work, and at other times gently pricking the bubble of conceit and laying out for the omniscient mind the work of a lifetime, but doing it so skilfully that the youth himself hardly knows how his self-satisfaction becomes transformed with the desire to learn more, far more than he ever knew before.[47]

That excellent results came from this seminar and the attendant circumstances at Clark University can hardly be questioned. Good selection of students there must have been; intelligent handling of graduate students was even more conspicuous. But nothing was permitted to interfere with quality. At the Decennial Celebration President Hall said: "One thing, at least, is true so far—hardship has no whit lowered our aims or diluted our quality, but if anything has had the reverse influence."

Restraint in Granting Degrees

The comparatively small number of degrees granted by the University is one indication of this maintenance of standards in spite of all difficulties. In the more than thirty years that elapsed between the opening of the University in 1889 and the date of Wilson's published list of Clark degrees (1920), the total of doctorates of philosophy was only 257, though Clark had been a purely graduate institution for half that period. Only 90 doctor's degrees had been conferred in the first fifteen years. One may judge something of the quality of the product by looking through the following names taken from the list of recipients of degrees.[48] The years in parentheses indicate the period of residence at Clark University, and the date given is that of the conferring of the doctor of philosophy degree:

MATHEMATICS

| J. W. A. Young | (1889–1892) | Sept. 16, 1892 |
| Frederick C. Ferry | (1895–1898) | June 15, 1898 |

PHYSICS

| Robert Hutchings Goddard | (1908–1911) | June 15, 1911 |

BIOLOGY

| Hermon C. Bumpus | (1889–1890) | Sept. 29, 1891 |

[47] From a letter in the collection *Quarter of a Century*, presented to Dr. Hall on the twenty-fifth anniversary of his presidency of Clark University.

[48] "List of Degrees Granted at Clark University and Clark College, 1889–1920." Compiled by Louis N. Wilson. *Publications of the Clark University Library*, vol. 6, no. 3, December, 1920, pp. 6 ff.

Psychology and Education

William L. Bryan	(Oct. 1891–Jan. 1893)	Dec. 13, 1892
Fletcher B. Dresslar	(1891–1892; Jan. 1893–1894)	June 14, 1894
Thaddeus L. Bolton	(1890–1893)	April 30, 1895
James H. Leuba	(1892–1895)	July 29, 1895
Ernest H. Lindley	(1895–1897)	June 12, 1897
A. Caswell Ellis	(1894–1897)	June 18, 1897
Edwin D. Starbuck	(1895–1897)	Aug. 3, 1897
Frederic Burk	(1896–1898)	June 8, 1898
Henry S. Curtis	(1895–1898)	June 16, 1898
Frederick E. Bolton	(1897–1898)	Aug. 15, 1898
Henry H. Goddard	(1896–1899)	June 12, 1899
Edmund B. Huey	(1897–1899)	July 15, 1899
Henry Davidson Sheldon	(1897–1900)	May 15, 1900
Frederick Eby	(1898–1900)	June 6, 1900
Willard S. Small	(1897–1900)	June 11, 1900
Edgar James Swift	(1901–1903)	June 16, 1903
Fred Kuhlmann	(1901–1903)	June 17, 1903
Edward Conradi	(1902–1904)	June 23, 1904
W. Fowler Bucke	(1902–1904)	June 24, 1904
Lewis Madison Terman	(1903–1905)	June 21, 1905
William F. Book	(1903–Feb., 1906)	June 19, 1906
Arnold Lucius Gesell	(1904–Dec., 1905; Apr., 1906–June, 1906)	June 19, 1906
George Edmund Myers	(1904–1906)	June 19, 1906
David Spence Hill	(1905–1907)	June 20, 1907
John Franklin Bobbitt	(1907–1909)	June 17, 1909
Howard W. Odum	(1908–1909)	June 17, 1909
Harry Woodburn Chase	(1908–1910)	June 16, 1910
William Henry Holmes, Jr.	(1909–1910)	June 16, 1910
Edward Ebenezer Weaver	(1908–1910)	June 16, 1910
Edmund Smith Conklin	(1908–1911)	June 15, 1911
Adele Adams Steele	(1910–1913)	June 17, 1913
Elizabeth Lindley Woods	(1910–1913)	June 17, 1913
Lawrence Augustus Averill	(1913–1915)	June 17, 1915
William Thomas Sanger	(1912–1913; Mar.–June, 1915)	June 17, 1915
Florence Mateer	(1913–1916)	June 15, 1916
Francis John O'Brien	(1912–1916)	June 15, 1916
Aubrey Augustus Douglass	(1914–1917)	June 19, 1917
Phyllis Mary Blanchard	(1917–1919)	June 23, 1919
Winifred V. Richmond	(1914–1916; Jan.–June, 1919)	June 23, 1919

Anthropology

Miriam VanWaters	(1910–1913)	June 17, 1913

Sociology

Iva Lowther Peters	(1917–1918)	June 20, 1918

History

Elizabeth Brett White	(1919–1920)	June 14, 1920

In the first dozen years of its existence Clark University provided nearly four hundred members of faculties and instructional staffs for colleges, universities, and normal schools, its graduates filling some of the most important posts in leading institutions. As with the Johns Hopkins, one was likely to find Clark men out in the pioneering places in higher education. And the early promise has persisted. At the 1937 meeting of a small group constituting the Board of Trustees of the Carnegie Foundation for the Advancement of Teaching—a group selected primarily for distinctive achievement in American higher education—four of the members present, all past or present heads of universities and colleges, had studied at Clark,[49] and three of them had received their doctor's degrees as the result of study at Clark University in the first ten years.

HALL'S PART IN THE CLARK SUCCESS

Dr. Tanner's statement in the letter previously quoted[50] with respect to Dr. Hall's pedagogical skill in the seminar suggests an inevitable question: To what extent was Hall's own personality responsible for the success of Clark University in accomplishing at least part of what it set out to do?

Any attempt to answer this question is complicated by the differences of opinion that have developed over the years regarding Dr. Hall's place in American education. Lorine Pruette says in her biography:

> By one evaluator he is estimated to have been "a negative force in experimental psychology," while another declares that "the chief contribution of G. Stanley Hall seems to me to be his true perspective of real experimental research in psychology."[51]

E. L. Thorndike maintained that Hall was essentially a literary man rather than a man of science, and artistic rather than matter-of-fact; that he was always interested in those aspects of philosophy, psychology, education, and religion "which did not involve detailed experimentation, intricate quantitative treatments of results, or rigor and subtlety of analysis."[52]

Following Hall's tremendous vogue in child psychology and adolescence

---

[49] President Frederick C. Ferry, Hamilton College; William L. Bryan, president-emeritus, Indiana University; Chancellor E. H. Lindley, University of Kansas; Chancellor Samuel P. Capen, University of Buffalo.

[50] Supra, pp. 79 f.

[51] Lorine Pruette, *G. Stanley Hall, a Biography of the Mind*, with an introduction by Carl Van Doren, New York, D. Appleton and Company, 1926, p. 195.

[52] *National Academy of Sciences*, vol. 12, pp. 135–154, 1929.

Dr. Amy Tanner says Hall's writing was, in his own mind, secondary to his teaching, that "practically

there ensued a long reaction, and it became fashionable in psychology text-books, especially at the height of the measurement epoch, to minimize what Hall had done and stigmatize it as "unscientific." At present many of the things Hall was most concerned about are again getting a hearing—in particular his insistence upon growth and development of human beings and his interest in a far wider application of psychology to life and education than has been customary in academic circles. Dr. Amy Tanner recalls a discussion as to the final value of his work in which Dr. Hall said, in effect, that he conceived his task as chiefly that of making the ground plans and beginning the foundations of what would some day be the science of psychology. "His main concern was that these foundations should be laid broad and deep and to that end he included in psychology much that others deemed doubtful. He knew well that much, perhaps even all, of his own work would be followed by more detailed and accurate work that would outdistance his, but he had no complaints on that score. Such work as his had to be done before the other work could be, and that sufficed him." [53]

But here we are particularly concerned with Hall's work in the field of graduate education in the large, not necessarily in psychology and education alone. Hall's "errancies" were obvious enough, President Bryan says,[54] and he was not a good administrator in the ordinarily accepted sense, "but in spite of that he did a remarkable thing at Clark." He was, says Dr. Bryan, "a great director of graduate work," inspiring students to rise to loftier heights than they otherwise would—though he was "grand" and "great" rather than precise and scholarly. Chancellor Capen, who was connected with both Clark College and Clark University, concurs in this impression.[55] Professor Blakeslee stresses Hall's versatility of mind, his keen intellectual curiosity, his ability to get students to realize their utmost possibilities. "Many a recognized scholar will state that his vision of an intellectual life came from G. Stanley Hall." Dean Henry D. Sheldon, of the University of Oregon, editor and compiler of Hall's letters, explains the early Clark success as largely due to Hall's personality, to the seminar, and to the enthusiasm of those who had studied at Clark—Earl Barnes, for example, on the Pacific Coast—in bringing Clark University to the attention of the right kind of

---

everything he wrote was done in the first place for his lectures," that he "never had the patience to work over his lecture material into any literary form for his books." (Letter of September 4, 1938.)

For a summary of the views of psychologists, see Starbuck's article in the *Psychological Review*, 32:103–120, March, 1925.

[53] Letter of September 4, 1938.

[54] Interview at Bloomington, Indiana, January 7, 1938.

[55] Letter of February 25, 1938.

students.[56] Sheldon characterized Hall in his article in the *Dictionary of American Biography* as "strong, sturdy, obstinate, and insatiably curious." He concedes that Hall was never looked upon by his contemporaries as an administrator; "his chief interests were in another direction." Hall's difficulties in personal relationships with faculty members have been mentioned in the account of the faculty resignations of 1892. Sheldon is inclined to believe, however, that if the Clark foundation had realized its original scope Hall might have turned out to be an educational administrator of a high order. Sheldon points out that Hall, during all the period of stress and strain at Clark University, was devoting himself to the new child-study movement and making a notable success of it, largely because of "his wide and thorough training, his ability as a public speaker, and his indefatigable energy in answering thousands of letters and in serving on innumerable committees." Speaking of Hall's return to the lecture room as head of the department of psychology, Sheldon says that as an "academic lecturer" he was uneven, "many of the aspects of the subject with which he had slight sympathy being passed over inadequately."

On the other hand, no lecturer could be clearer or more forceful or richer in suggestions in dealing with the topics which suited his own view of life. His great strength as an academic teacher came out in his seminar. . . . As a popular lecturer to teachers' gatherings and at summer schools he was at his best.[57]

Students the Chief Concern

His students were the main thing, says Dr. Tanner. "Every day from two to six they were welcome at his house, where he took them to his study, talked over their theses and courses, gave them references, sized them up, and every now and then struck out a spark that that man kept lighted for the rest of his life. Nothing was so interesting to Dr. Hall as another person, and when that person was also one who had come to him to learn, there was almost literally no limit to the time and patience and wisdom that he would give. Rare indeed was the student who did not respond to the limit of his abilities."

Nor was he concerned that the student should agree with him. Dr. Tanner tells of one woman whose Ph.D. thesis contained conclusions that Dr. Hall believed erroneous, so much so that he used all his persuasiveness to change her mind besides overwhelming her with references. "He could not change

---

[56] From an interview at Eugene, Oregon, July 10, 1938.

[57] *Dictionary of American Biography*, vol. VIII, p. 129.

her mind," says Dr. Tanner, "but he accepted her thesis and printed it in one of his magazines, and certainly that young woman had learned to defend her opinions and incidentally had a knowledge of her subject that few aspirants to the Ph.D. have."[58]

Edmund Sanford, who helped substantially in drawing together Clark University and Clark College after the founder's will had necessitated the establishment of the separate college, and who has put on record his conviction that Dr. Hall won at Clark "a victory out of defeat," cites as one of the chief characteristics of Hall's work "the relative absence from it of anything like systematization." His own thought was too fresh, too full of nascent possibilities, Sanford says, to permit him to lay it out in regularly concatenated sequences. "His natural bent was creative rather than critical." He was a typical *Romantiker* in science:

> His teaching, his public lecturing, the variety of new problems which he considered, his output of papers, his carelessness of details and minor errors, which the care of his devoted assistants could not wholly eliminate, the unmistakable character of his writing (the "Hall" mark so easily recognized), the extent of his early influence upon the development of psychology in America and throughout his career upon education—one and all run true to type. It is as a pioneer and propagandist in these fields that he must be judged. The attempt to appraise him by other standards misses the essential meaning and purpose of his life.[59]

It is also likely, Sanford thinks, that Hall's scientific contributions will suffer the typical fate of the work of the romanticist in any field. He points out that the specific things with which Hall's name was associated have already been "revised or superseded by the more accurate surveys of later comers"—a result which Dr. Hall, like any true *Romantiker*, would have looked forward to with entire equanimity. "But the larger principles which underlay his work—none of them indeed original with him nor exclusively his, yet all held enthusiastically by him and greatly advanced by his support—the belief in research, the genetic point of view in psychology, the psychological point of view in education and religion, the importance of studying children and young people as the key to teaching them, the passionate reverence for youth, health, freedom, and self-realization—his contribution to the effective recognition of all these and to their progressive realization in

[58] Letter of September 4, 1938.

[59] Edmund C. Sanford, "Granville Stanley Hall," *Publications of Clark University Library*, vol. 7, no. 6, May, 1925, p. 41.

action nothing can ever lessen or gainsay; it has already passed into the vital current of the time." And he adds:

> To preach and to practice such principles as these is the work of a great teacher; and it is as a great teacher—not merely of graduate students or of the general public—but as the inspired seer and prophet of a genuine psychological and educational gospel that his place and reputation are secure. To those who were his pupils, the inspiration, the illumination, the friendliness are unforgettable. While these pupils live his memory will live also. When they are gone, and those also who found inspiration in his more publicly spoken word, his books may lose in power and the lustre of his name grow dim, but none the less his nameless influence will still be making powerfully everywhere for the advantage of the things which he most loved: youth, freedom, new knowledge.

Pioneering in a New Science

William H. Burnham notes that just as in his professional activities Hall refused to waste his time with red tape and the details of an academic machine, "so he refused to waste his mental energy in thinking of the trivial and the unessential." The point is, says Burnham, "that he did it; others seldom have done it." Dr. Sarah C. Fisher, in her discussion of Hall's work, agrees with other commentators that Hall probably found the type of work which would give his genius the best expression, that of "pioneer and prophet of a young and growing science sufficiently related to practical needs to offer opportunity for the enthusiastic propagandist."

> Here he could perform his most brilliant and distinguished service. Here lack of system was the least handicap, for the times were not ripe for system in psychology. His chief temperamental needs were socially polarized —to extend, to impress, students and others, to apply, to create opportunities for freedom and avenues for publication of work; and for this his style was supremely fitted. He was rarely equipped for the task of "generating interest over a large surface," which the worker, with his problems upon him, can turn into a narrow outlet; and from workers in the field of education have come the most enthusiastic tributes. Hall, the "passionate lover" of youth and childhood, has served youth more than anything else, and especially handicapped, adult-ridden youth. There is no field of education but has felt the influence emanating from him and has been markedly benefited; and if every worker who is concerned with the handling of childhood and adolescence were familiar with the assembled information, tenets, and spirit of Hall's writings, a mighty stride would be taken toward

the solution of the problems of criminology and a new day would dawn for youth.[60]

Lorine Pruette tells of the last Founder's Day which Hall was to see, in February, 1923, when the former president was asked to speak to the students. He talked on the subject of judging men and described his own particular scale by means of which he evaluated others. Says Dr. Pruette:

> This was perhaps the last signal demonstration of the peculiar power which he had over his listeners, for in this address he reverted almost completely to his classroom manner. His manuscript lay before him on a high "pulpit," it was necessary for him to bring his eyes very close to the typed page from which he read, and the reading was accomplished by means of sharp little darts into the manuscript and up again. As usual he was in tremendous haste; his words were poured out as if some inexorable figure would surely call on him before he was half finished; his reading was expressionless except for odd bits of emphasis upon the ends of sentences, which he sometimes brought out vigorously in a sort of triumphant fervor. On he hastened, sweeping his hearers along upon a stream of words half understood, giving them fleeting glimpses of great ideas, out of the commonplace things of life building for them a new exultation and a new hope. The college boys came away declaring that they would never forget that hour. They had sat at the feet of a master of persuasion; they had peered, fascinated, into their own souls, and had glimpsed there untold riches which a lifetime would be all too short to realize.[61]

Most of the comments just cited have had to do with Hall's place in psychology and education rather than in graduate work specifically. Somewhat more applicable to university education, but still ranging over all levels, is President Eliot's statement before the New England Association of Colleges and Secondary Schools in 1901: "With regard to President Hall's contribution, it is, like almost all his contributions to the study of education, a powerful helper toward freedom, toward the realization of the content in education instead of the form, toward the reduction of an undue amount of method and schedule and control. It means, like all his work, more freedom for the child. . . . His whole service to education seems to me to be in the right direction, and his contributions, therefore, have always been peculiarly welcome to me. I hope I had a little bit to do with the first evidences of skill and knowledge which President Hall gave to the public."[62]

[60] Sarah Carolyn Fisher, "The Psychological and Educational Work of Granville Stanley Hall," *American Journal of Psychology*, 36:1–52, January, 1925.

[61] Lorine Pruette, *G. Stanley Hall: A Biography of the Mind*, pp. 161–162.

[62] *School Review*, December, 1901, p. 680.

The Human Factor

To return, then, to the specific question as to Hall's place in the Clark University experience, it would seem to be necessary to assign a large part of the successes as well as the difficulties, to Dr. Hall himself. This is only another way of emphasizing, however, the human factor as the first essential in any educational enterprise. Indeed, Professor E. D. Starbuck in summarizing the views of psychologists with respect to Hall's contribution points out that a significant fact about Hall was that *his own values centered in persons.* "He was himself, first and foremost, a radiating and vitalizing personality. He was 'a vital contact.' 'You could talk with him.' 'He prevented more human shipwrecks than any teacher I have ever known.' 'He did not teach me *how* to work or think, or *what* to think, but he gave me the conviction and courage that one must dare to do his own thinking, that intellectual salvation grounds in that principle."[63]

Moreover, as indicated or implied at various points in these pages, Dr. Hall was by no means the only "personality" in the Clark story. Not only were there a host of able scholars, teachers, and research workers in the Worcester group at the different periods, but a considerable proportion of them seem to have been, as so many university teachers have not been, humanly interesting people. Multiplication of graduate facilities has doubtless been one of the important reasons for the apparent scarcity of superior personalities in university and college teaching, particularly at the graduate level, but that is not the only reason—a pattern has been developed, and it has almost become the fashion for university teaching to be literal and unimaginative rather than colorful and inspired. We have shunned the interesting for fear it would not be scientific; otherwise it is difficult to account for the stacks of dull and unimportant theses that have piled up over the years. The Clark doctoral dissertations may have been superseded and the findings may often be questionable today, but there is a vitality and emotional quality about them that even now make one who reads them feel that the young authors were really searching for truth, not just performing a chore; that they were working with scientists and teachers who were not so completely scientific but that they could be deeply concerned with the human and social implications of research findings.

Dr. Sanford suggests part of the answer to the question of Dr. Hall's place in the total Clark story when he wonders, in describing the outdis-

[63] Edwin Dillon Starbuck, "G. Stanley Hall," *Psychological Review*, 32:119, March, 1925. Also given in Thorndike, "Biographical Memoir of Granville Stanley Hall," National Academy of Sciences, 12:135–154 (Washington, D. C., *The Academy*, 1929).

tancing of Clark by universities with greater resources in the period just before 1920, "how long any students at all would forego the attractions of the richer institutions for the close personal contact of students and professor which was the chief advantage Clark now had to offer."[64] This surviving advantage was a real one. Professor Sanford would undoubtedly have granted that intimate personal relationship is still possible in some departments today at very large universities but, if student opinion is to be believed, on the whole this type of relationship is conspicuously lacking. There seems to be justification for the impression that huge numbers do generally result in elaborate machinery and organization, and that these in turn make it very difficult for even those research workers most concerned with individual students to carry out their ideals; while even in smaller institutions, where one would expect the lack of huge enrollments to encourage the kind of learning relationship found so valuable at Hopkins and Clark, habits formed at the larger centers seem to persist, and only in rare instances do the faculty grasp their opportunity to do what the staffs at Hopkins and Clark did. The special Clark contribution to this problem lay not only in small numbers and close personal relations between faculty and students, but also in having as leader a man whose disposition was to keep the human side of a university enterprise uppermost and therefore comparatively free from the elaborate organizational and administrative machinery that interferes with personal relationships in education.

It is perhaps fair to say, then, that G. Stanley Hall himself may not have been essential to the success of Clark University, but that the achievement would not have been possible without someone at the head who had an equal concern for human rather than material values.

OTHER ELEMENTS IN THE CLARK ACHIEVEMENT

Other factors were present, of course, in the Clark experience besides those that have been emphasized in the present account. President Hall on various occasions spoke in high praise of the Clark University Board of Trustees, the members of which did go along with their educational leader, even if the founder did not. They were not only outstanding men of their day, but they seem to have understood the philosophy that ought to animate such boards—that of maintaining a policy-making function, in which the board is aided and advised by its professional director but keeps clear of entanglements in the details of administration.

[64] Edmund C. Sanford, "A Sketch of the History of Clark University," p. 8.

As at Hopkins, the journals and other publications played an important part. In 1891 Dr. Hall started at his own expense the *Pedagogical Seminary*, a quarterly printing six hundred pages a year, in the first volumes of which many of the contributions were from Clark University or Hall's own pen. It is worth noting that in the commemorative volume of twenty-five articles by eminent American and European psychologists published in 1903, Hall is signalized as not only the originator of the first laboratory of experimental psychology in America, but also as "founder of the first American journal for the publication of the results of psychological investigation."[65] The editorial note in the first issue of this journal explained that its object was "to record the psychological work of a scientific, as distinct from a speculative character, which has been so widely scattered as to be largely inaccessible save to a very few, and often overlooked by them."

It is the principle of creative research and adequate publication for it that is important here, not the particular form of publication or implementation. A journal of the type used so effectively at Hopkins, Clark, and Chicago in the past may not be the answer at all today, but the task of making research findings known and acted upon is more important than ever.

Throughout the Clark University development a few rather simple elements stand forth: Designation at the start of an educational leader with a background of rich experience, powerful drive, and a broad philosophy of education; a determination to build on the basis of ascertained needs rather than traditional academic patterns; careful selection of teaching staff and students in the light of these needs, with emphasis upon "creative" learning and research of graduate quality because that area was not then occupied to any large extent by other higher institutions; an informal relationship between faculty and students, in which the cooperative possibilities of the search for truth were emphasized, culminating in a surpassingly effective use of the "seminar" in which were combined the features of coordinated planning and pooled experiences, independent exploration into a wide variety of fields of knowledge, inspired direction of the advanced work of mature students, and magnificent lecturing of an unconventional order.

Some of these were specific for Clark University as to time and place; but most of them involve principles that would have significance for any educational program, especially at the graduate level.

[65] Commemorative issue of the *American Journal of Psychology*, October, 1903.

III

EARLY GRADUATE WORK
AT THE UNIVERSITY OF CHICAGO

President Harper . . . had to mediate and compromise between a divinity school and a faculty to whose members he had promised entire academic freedom, and the spokesman of an alarmed sectarian orthodoxy; between the requirements of an ideal for the University that constantly outran its budget, and the practical business sense of trustees and founders for whom living within an income was the first test of sound administration; between a public for whom a college was a school, and a band of scholars whose hearts were set upon research; between the promoters of immediate expansion into professional schools of every kind, with whom his own impatience sympathized, and the cautious advocates of consolidation within departments already established.

Professor PAUL SHOREY, article on Harper
in the *Dictionary of American Biography*

WILLIAM RAINEY HARPER was as clear in his own mind as Daniel C. Gilman and G. Stanley Hall had been in theirs that the new institution to be set going at Chicago was to be a departure—a unique departure, he believed—in American education. "Until the founding of Johns Hopkins University," he said in his address to the third convocation, June, 1893, "there was but one type of college in America. No institution doing real university work existed. With the establishment of the University of Chicago another type, it is believed, has been introduced, differing essentially from the college of historic character, and, just as essentially, from the type of Johns Hopkins."

Nominally it was a "college" rather than a university that was initiated at Chicago in 1890. Mr. John D. Rockefeller's letter to Dr. Frederick T. Gates of May 15, 1889, announcing his offer says explicitly: "I will contribute six hundred thousand dollars toward an endowment fund for a college." Behind the careful use of the term "college" in this communication, however, there was a long story of negotiation that involved expediency as well as educational policy. President Harper's own statements leave no doubt as to where he stood with respect to the work the institution was to do. In a document prepared a few months before the University opened he stressed the point that it was proposed to establish, not a college, but a university. "A large number of the professors have been selected with the understanding that their work is to be exclusively in the graduate schools," he said. The purpose was to help existing colleges, not to compete with them; accordingly, "the main energies of the institution have been directed toward graduate work."

What was there, then, about the University of Chicago, in its origin and early history, to justify for it Dr. Harper's claim of uniqueness in the field of university graduate work?

HISTORY OF THE UNIVERSITY

An earlier University of Chicago existed from 1859 to 1886. Originating in a grant by Senator Stephen A. Douglas of some ten acres of land "for a site for a university in the city of Chicago," it had been established by the Baptist denomination and maintained by this religious group through years of almost incredible financial difficulty. In 1861 it included an "academy," with ninety-nine students, a "college" with a total of forty-nine in the "classical" and "scientific" courses, a two-year agricultural department (temporarily in abeyance), and a law department with thirty-six enrolled. The value of its first large public subscription wiped out by the panic of 1857, fundraising made impossible by the Civil War, and such resources as it might have clung to destroyed in the successive calamities of the great fire of 1871, the panic of 1873, and the second big fire of 1874, the institution finally succumbed in 1886. "Notwithstanding its unfortunate fiscal history," Thomas Wakefield Goodspeed says, "the old University had an interesting and fruitful educational career."[1]

The Baptists of Chicago could not reconcile themselves to the loss of the University. Even before its demise they were planning another. The Baptist Union Theological Seminary continued to operate vigorously, and "it was a thing not to be thought of that there should not exist a college or university" in immediate proximity to it. Mr. John D. Rockefeller had become a regular benefactor of the Seminary, then located at Morgan Park, Illinois, and Dr. Thomas W. Goodspeed, who was secretary and financial representative of the institution from 1876 to 1889, is generally credited with having been the man who first drew Mr. Rockefeller's attention to the need of a powerful Baptist educational enterprise at Chicago.[2]

At this same period the Reverend Augustus H. Strong, President of the Rochester, New York, Theological Seminary, a prominent Baptist clergyman who had been Mr. Rockefeller's pastor when the latter was a rising

[1] The figures are from the annual catalogues of the old University for the years indicated. Thomas Wakefield Goodspeed's accounts are in his *A History of the University of Chicago* (Chicago, University of Chicago Press, 1916) and his shorter *The Story of the University of Chicago* (Chicago, University of Chicago Press, 1925), both of which have been drawn upon in preparing the brief historical summary in this section. For the discussion of the events which led to the grants from Mr. Rockefeller the chief source has been the Harper correspondence in the President's office at the University of Chicago.

[2] Editor's note prefixed to the Harper correspondence.

young business man in Cleveland, Ohio, and whose oldest son had married Mr. Rockefeller's oldest daughter, was using every possible means to enlist Mr. Rockefeller's support for a $20,000,000 university under Baptist auspices in New York City. It was these conflicting pressures, the now available Harper correspondence reveals most clearly (pressures apparently exerted by one group without knowledge that corresponding efforts were being made by the other) that harassed Mr. Rockefeller, delayed action on possible educational plans, and dictated to some extent the character of the new institution, or at least the form in which it was first to be presented.[3]

This is not the place to give in any detail the long-drawn-out controversy over the location of the proposed Baptist university—as to whether it should be in New York, Washington, or Chicago; but the letters written between 1886 and 1890 by the group of men most vitally concerned—Frederick T. Gates, then corresponding secretary of the American Baptist Education Society and afterward chairman of the General Education Board, Thomas Wakefield Goodspeed, William Rainey Harper, G. W. Northrup of the Baptist Seminary, Henry L. Morehouse, corresponding secretary of the American Baptist Home Mission Society, Augustus H. Strong, and Mr. Rockefeller himself—are important because they give a vivid and at times dramatic picture of the conditions under which the Chicago university project developed and the kind of institution that was contemplated by those who campaigned for it.

WHAT A UNIVERSITY IS

In one of the first of the papers in the Harper collection Dr. Strong sets forth his notion of what a university is and why the Baptists must have one. "A university in the proper sense," he wrote in 1886, "is an institution for advanced and professional studies"—advanced in distinction from studies that are "merely elementary and intended for purposes of mental discipline," professional in contrast to those that are merely general and "incident to all liberal education." Using much the same arguments that Presidents Gilman and Hall had used, Dr. Strong pointed out that the true universities of his day were found only in Europe. He cited the University of Berlin with its five thousand students, all with a complete "college" or *gymnasium* training before entrance upon university work, and Oxford and Cambridge with their

---

[3] "I was writing in behalf of Chicago quite unconscious of this very powerful contrary influence." (Thomas W. Goodspeed, *The Story of the University of Chicago*, p. 10.) Dr. George E. Vincent's statement in the proceedings of the William Rainey Harper Memorial Conference, p. 8, also describes the situation in part.

twenty-five hundred to three thousand students. In the United States, he said, only the beginnings of true university education were discernible; of Harvard's fifteen hundred students, all but five hundred belonged in the college and were not properly university students at all, and of Harvard's ten million dollars worth of property not more than a million was applicable to real university purposes. Even Johns Hopkins, at Baltimore, which came "nearest to a university of anything in America," gave genuine advanced instruction, and furnished faculty members for both Harvard and Yale, had nevertheless, he asserted, been weakened by the retention of a college department for local students.

Not only did the Baptists entirely lack a university of the right sort, Dr. Strong said, but there was "no university at all in New York." A real university, he insisted, should have a comprehensive fellowship system as the central feature. He contrasted the huge endowments for fellowship and scholarship aids in England—311 fellowships and 436 scholarships at Oxford and 335 fellowships and 795 scholarships at Cambridge, all on good stipends —with the ten fellowships available at Harvard and the twenty at Johns Hopkins.

Early in the exchange of letters Goodspeed wrote to Mr. Rockefeller describing how the Baptists of the Chicago area felt at losing Professor William Rainey Harper, then on the Seminary faculty, to Yale, and recording their hope that Harper might head a reestablished University of Chicago:

> Dr. Northrup says he has greater capabilities than any man he knows. . . . He is now, at thirty years of age . . . not only a scholar, but a leader, an organizer, an administrator, and is easily first and chief in all these directions. He has immense capacity for work and for bringing things to pass. He is now teaching 1,000 men by correspondence. He has organized the Hebrew professors of all the seminaries of the country, is conducting six summer schools of Hebrew, with these professors—many of them eminent men—working under him. . . .
>
> We have proposed to Dr. Harper to assume the presidency of our wrecked and ruined university and reestablish it here at Morgan Park. . . .
>
> This great center is the place above all others for building up a great and powerful university. . . .
>
> Our seminary can no more hold him long within its limits than your first refinery could hold you—if you will pardon the comparison. . . . We have not so many men of eminent abilities that we can spare such a man to Yale and the Congregationalists.

Mr. Rockefeller did not respond very actively to the first suggestions made for a university at Chicago. "There is hardly a chance that I could give the least encouragement for assistance in respect to the university," he wrote on December 31, 1886, to Goodspeed, but he added that he would carefully read a communication with regard to it. Then, in rapid succession, came a series of letters from both Chicago and New York. "We should have a new institution in New York," wrote Strong to Rockefeller, January 4, 1887. From Chicago, Goodspeed to Rockefeller, January 7th: "We desire to found here a new university." On January 11th Dr. Harper wrote to Mr. Rockefeller approving of Goodspeed's suggestion; the more he saw of Eastern institutions, he said, the more he felt that there was "no greater work to be done on this continent than the work of establishing a university in or near Chicago." Speaking, he says, as an entirely disinterested person (because of his recently announced appointment to Yale), he considered it "safe to make the prediction that in ten years such a university would have more students, if rightly conducted, than Harvard or Yale has today."

On February 14th Mr. Rockefeller said he would "still further investigate." The same day he sent to Dr. Strong the letters from Goodspeed and Harper about a university in Chicago with the note: "Say to me in confidence what you think of it." Strong replied immediately that "next to New York" he was interested in seeing something done for Chicago; he was "happy to commend Dr. Goodspeed's plan," except that the amount seemed to him ridiculously small—"we are already burdened with too many starveling institutions that divide our strength and degrade our scholarship." A few days later Mr. Rockefeller wrote to Dr. Strong:

> I am willing to take up the question, when our Baptist people are ready, of an educational institution in New York, and suppose that the additional endowment proposed for Rochester could be utilized for this purpose, could we succeed in centralizing here later.

A Baptist Enterprise

It was still very much a Baptist university that was under consideration East and West. Strong transmitted to Rockefeller, from February 22, 1887 on, a series of statements about his plan, in the first of which he said:

> What moves me is the simple consideration that we Baptists, with two millions and a half of members and ten millions of constituency, are so unspeakably behindhand in matters of education, are making so insufficient provision for the future, are letting other smaller bodies of Christians go so far ahead of us, are losing day by day so many of our best and

brightest men because we have no proper facilities for their education. We have no theological seminary that has a quarter of the strength of the Union Seminary in New York. We have no college that has a tenth of the influence or equipment of Harvard or Yale. So our young men go to Harvard and Yale and Princeton, and—leave the Baptist ranks. So our instructors, like Harper and Wheeler and Stevens, are enticed to other institutions. We need a first class college and seminary more than we need anything else, and we need it in New York. . . .

We need an institution which shall be truly a university, where, as at Johns Hopkins, there shall be a large number of fellowships, where research shall be endowed, where the brightest men shall be attracted and helped through their studies, where the institution itself shall furnish a real society of people distinguished in science and art. And of such a university, the theological school should be the center, giving aim and character to all the rest.

Dr. Strong argued that the denomination would never be able to initiate such an enterprise; it would have to depend upon an individual gift. He appealed personally to Mr. Rockefeller:

Would it not make the noblest work as well as the noblest recreation of the remainder of your life if, not neglecting other and distant interests, you should devote yourself mainly to the travel and investigation connected with the establishment of an institution in New York such as the country does not now possess?

Could you give your son a nobler education during the next ten years than to have him grow up amid the discussions and interviews connected with such a plan? . . . I should like to know whether the court will hear further argument.

And he emphasized that what he had in mind was a *university proper*, an institution for advanced students only, for those who have finished their college course, an institution after the larger European plan, "such as Johns Hopkins University is seeking to be in this country," the fundamental idea of which would be endowment of higher education and research.

He continued to stress, however, the denominational character of the proposed institution. The fellowships would be awarded each year "to the graduates of all our Baptist colleges throughout the land"; all the work of the University should be "Christian, based upon the Bible," and should center around advanced training for the ministry, but the training should be so advanced that graduates of other theological seminaries would come to it.

I would admit none but exceptionally prepared men, and that only after rigid examination; then I would give them the chance to pursue their studies further than can now be done except by going to Europe. . . .

Bricks and mortar, the erection of buildings, should be the last thing. Temporary accommodations will answer, as at Johns Hopkins, until the thing gets a good start. . . . Then buildings could be put up as need arose. . . . The possibility of doing this sort of thing has been demonstrated already at Baltimore—a very poor location compared with New York.

To this barrage Mr. Rockefeller responded on March 22, 1887:

I have all your communications in respect to the university at New York and we will have opportunity to talk in reference to the same before long. There is nothing new in my mind in respect to it.

From Chicago the prodding also went on. Goodspeed, writing under date of May 7, 1887, thought it was "an unspeakable calamity that we have no respectable Baptist college in the West"—but, he added, "you are not responsible for it, nor can I lay it now upon you." Mr. Rockefeller remained lukewarm, but willing to listen, answering Goodspeed that he "continued to think and talk in regard to the Chicago university," but did not feel hopeful that he could give any encouragement. He was about to start on a trip for Europe on which Dr. Strong accompanied him.

In the fall the attack was resumed from both New York and Chicago, this time taking its point from the fact that Harper was likely to be lost to the Baptist cause. Dr. Strong himself wrote Mr. Rockefeller, on September 24, 1887, that he had seen Professor Harper and had acquainted him with the main features of the Strong plan for a university in New York. "My dear Mr. Rockefeller," Strong wrote on this occasion, "if we let that man go out of our hands it will be the greatest loss our denomination has sustained during this century. . . . President Dwight has been talking to him about the slightness of the differences between Baptists and Congregationalists in a way that is distasteful to him." The next day he informed Mr. Rockefeller that—

President Dwight and his helpers at Yale are now engaged in a great effort to raise two millions of dollars to endow postgraduate instruction in the university, and the larger part of it is already raised and is to be devoted to the school of languages, etc., of which Professor Harper is invited to be the head. . . . Now he [Harper] does not want to get away from theological work and he does not want to get away from his own denomination if he can help it. But he is young and of immense energy, and he feels that he must take the place where he can do the most, even if it be out of denominational lines.

A few days later Strong was again harping on the same theme: New York City was bound to have advanced and professional instruction—the only question was "whether we shall let other denominations do our work and take our men away from us, while we lose both the city and the country too. My soul is burdened with the matter; may God give you his own wisdom." Some days later he was once more distressed over Harper and the "good Congregational brethren so anxious to get him committeed to permanent service at Yale" that they were willing to help him in one of his most cherished ambitions, that of promoting the study of the Old Testament Scriptures.

By November, 1887, Strong was pushing Mr. Rockefeller harder than ever and beginning to show impatience. He wrote: "You have the opportunity of turning the unfavorable judgments of the world at large into favorable judgments, and not only that, but of going down to history as one of the world's greatest benefactors." And he concludes: "I feel as if I could hardly go through the strain of meditating and praying about this for another year. I had almost rather leave my testimony and die."

This was all getting too tense for Mr. Rockefeller. On November 30, 1887, he wrote Dr. Strong: "I have decided to indefinitely postpone the consideration of the question of the university or theological seminary in New York." And when Dr. Harper the following month asked what he should say in Chicago about the matter of the university at New York, since he did not wish to seem "unpleasantly silent," Mr. Rockefeller replied that nothing definite had been arrived at.

A few months later, bothered by premature reports that he was going to do something for Chicago, Mr. Rockefeller wrote George C. Lorimer that "the report was incorrect about my being connected with the effort to establish a university at Chicago," that he was so heavily weighted with other undertakings he could give no encouragement in that direction. Dr. Strong's letter of February 26, 1888, however, written after he had twice seen Mr. Rockefeller, informed Dr. Harper that "the thing is working, and is coming out all right. . . . I go back tonight much more sure that we are approaching a favorable conclusion." Three months after this, in May, 1888, Dr. Strong was writing to Mr. Rockefeller a description of an interview he had just had with President Daniel C. Gilman at Baltimore, in which, he declared, the Johns Hopkins head had enthusiastically approved the idea of the university at New York. Mr. Rockefeller's comment with regard to Gilman was brief— "he must be something of a man!" Mr. Rockefeller, however, was still very resistant toward Chicago. He answered a despairing plea from Goodspeed in July, 1888, by saying he could do nothing, and he not only had his secretary write to the same effect to George C. Lorimer, but he even declined to grant an interview at Cleveland with regard to the matter.

Mr. Rockefeller and Dr. Harper

It was in October of 1888 that the decisive turn came, and, as Mr. Rockefeller afterward stated in a letter, it was the direct result of Dr. Harper's interest and activity. Dr. Harper and Mr. Rockefeller had been together the better part of two days at Vassar College and on the train going back to New York. Harper found that Mr. Rockefeller had become "somewhat exasperated" by the attitude of the Chicago men with reference to the Chicago university. He felt that they did not treat him justly, and he had decided not to have anything to do with the affair. "But now he stands ready after the holidays to do something for Chicago. It will have to be managed, however, very carefully." Mr. Rockefeller's mind had turned, Harper felt confident, and "it is a possible thing to have the money which he proposed to spend in New York diverted to Chicago." Mr. Rockefeller himself, Harper reported, "made out a list of reasons why it would be better to go to Chicago than to remain in New York." Harper warned, however, that "we must not expect too much; we all know how easy it is to make a start and then fall back."[4]

In the meantime Dr. Gates had read before the Baptist Ministers' Conference at Chicago a paper on "A New University in Chicago a Denominational Necessity, as Illustrated by a Study of Western Baptist Collegiate Education." This had a tremendous effect upon the Baptist group. In Dr. Gates's own words, "The brethren were 'all torn up' over it. They were astonished, astounded, confounded, dumbfounded, amazed, bewildered, overwhelmed" at the picture given of the weakness of western education and the evidence of the need for a great university at Chicago. Goodspeed, asking Gates for a copy of the paper, said it had "stirred his heart"—he wanted it to "stir another's heart." The paper was uncompromising in its revelation of the poverty and meagerness of Baptist higher education: "Our colleges are unevenly distributed, feeble in resources, narrow in area of attractive influence, and obscurely located. As compared with either of the other three largest Protestant denominations, our education work is merely fractional." Of many things that must be done to remedy the conditions, Dr. Gates said, the first and most important was "to found a great college, ultimately to be a university, in Chicago."

---

[4] This letter is given in part in Thomas W. Goodspeed, *The Story of the University of Chicago*, pp. 14–15.

We need in Chicago an institution with an endowment of several millions, with buildings, library, and other appliances equal to any on the continent; an institution commanding the services of the ablest specialists in every department, giving the highest classical as well as scientific culture, and aiming to counteract the western tendency to a merely superficial and utilitarian education—an institution wholly under Baptist control as a chartered right, loyal to Christ and His Church, employing none but Christians in any department of instruction, a school not only evangelical but evangelistic, seeking to bring every student into surrender to Jesus Christ as Lord.

Such an institution should be located in Chicago, because this city is the most commanding social, financial, literary, and religious eminence in the West. . . . Chicago is the heart of the West, the fountain of western life. . . . All roads lead to Chicago. All cities, all rural homes face Chicago. . . . Between the Allegheny and the Rocky mountains there is not to be found another city in which such an institution as we need could be established, or if established could be maintained and enlarged, or if maintained could achieve wide influence or retain supremacy among us. . . . I can imagine no educational work which would at once remove so many difficulties, restore so many disaffections, reduce to harmony and order so many chaotic elements, meet needs so wide, so deep, and so immediate, or confer so large a boon on the cause of Christ in the West. Nothing great or worthy can be achieved or attempted for education in the West until this thing is done.

Mr. Rockefeller quite evidently was "stirred" by the Gates report. On November 5, 1888, Harper was able to write to Goodspeed, following another long session of many hours with Mr. Rockefeller at Poughkeepsie, "It is absolutely certain that the thing is to be done; it is now only a question as to what scale." Within a few days Mr. Goodspeed was in New York at Mr. Rockefeller's telegraphed request to discuss the new university in Chicago. "It must be borne in mind," says Mr. Goodspeed in reporting the episode later in his history, "that Dr. Harper had never had in mind anything less than a real university, with colleges and graduate departments. He had impressed this upon me in his letters and took occasion to do this again in our interview together Friday evening. I, on the other hand, had been for more than two years asking Mr. Rockefeller's help in founding a college."[5]

New York or Chicago?

By November 14th Gates was in a position to say that "Mr. Rockefeller

[5] Ibid., p. 16.

has definitely abandoned all present thought of Dr. Strong's scheme, and has made up his mind to endow a college in Chicago and other western colleges at strategic points in the future." Once Dr. Strong began to realize that the prospective donor was turning his mind westward, he put forth unusual efforts to save the New York proposal. He wrote Dr. Harper that he felt he, Harper, was in error in advising Mr. Rockefeller to separate theology from the other departments of the university and to put the university at Chicago. Chicago, he conceded, was the place for a first class college, but not for a real university:

Chicago is not the place for a university which is to command the patronage of all the States East and West, and to send out influence throughout the world. . . .

Remember that a true university is an institution solely for advanced and professional instruction, and that it requires for feeders a number of subordinate colleges. Our colleges are all at the East. We ought not to put our university far away from the base of supplies. . . . The graduates of neither Baptist nor non-Baptist colleges at the East would go so far away as Chicago to take university instruction; they will stop at the professional schools nearer home. It would take many years to raise up feeders at the West. In the meantime, there would be the strongest temptation to add to the university an academic and collegiate department as a sort of preparatory school. This would at once take the so-called university out of the category of universities proper, and subject it perpetually to all the hampering limitations which now affect Yale and Harvard. The greatest chance ever offered in American education, as Dr. Gilman of Johns Hopkins told me, is the chance now open to establish a true university in New York. The doing of it will make the founder famous to all ages.

Strong argued that locating the university at Chicago would needlessly divide the available resources; moreover, "theology absolutely needs the other departments of a university to broaden it, while the other departments need theology as a standard and *terminus ad quem*." New York was the eye of America, as Athens was the eye of Greece. Commercially and politically, educationally and religiously, Strong maintained, New York led and would continue to lead the continent:

While the chance is open to us to take possession of New York, and to lead the march of education on this continent, it would be the greatest pity to take up with a second-best location. That is what Baptists hitherto have always been doing—building their churches on the back streets, and their colleges in the country towns. Let us have an end of this once for all. The taking of New York, by the grandest educational enterprise on the continent, would put heart and hope into our whole Baptist body, while the establishment of a mongrel institution in Chicago, which is neither fish, flesh, nor fowl, neither university, college, nor academy, but all three combined, would create no more of a ripple on the surface of our educational ocean than the work of Madison University now does. . . . We have already enough one-horse colleges to stock the world—so far as numbers are concerned. Let us not so divide up our funds as to add to the numbers of such. They degrade our education and disgrace our denomination.

He added, in a postscript:

A university, as has been said by another, needs more than money. It needs libraries, museums, and especially *men.* The students of the professions need to see men, and to hear them. They need to feel the force of the strongest currents of modern life, and to be in the midst of its most intense activities. These advantages are found in New York as they are not found in Chicago. For this reason New York will have a drawing power that Chicago will not have. . . . *Distance* amounts to little nowadays. *Direction* amounts to a great deal. Men will go east when they will not go west. New York can draw students from the extremes of the country. It would be cheaper to pay railroad fares for all students from the Pacific Coast to New York than to establish a university in San Francisco. The same argument applies to Chicago. An institution at Chicago must of necessity be provincial and sectional, while in New York it would be both *national* and *international.*

Dr. Harper promptly communicated to Mr. Rockefeller the contents of the Strong letter and suggested that he ask Dr. Strong for his views. Goodspeed wrote to Harper, November 24th, in substance: "Very well, give us a college and it's bound to grow any way"; to which Harper retorted that they must insist upon something as large as possible; that "unless we hold a stiff upper lip and come out boldly and confidently for what we want, viz., *a university of the highest character* . . . we shall lose ground and make a mistake." On November 29 Harper sent Rockefeller clippings showing that plans were being discussed for a *secular* university and gave it as his opinion that there was real risk that such a university might be established if their own plans could not be carried through.

In the meantime, Dr. Strong, seeing his New York plans about to be lost, became "desperate," as Harper informed Goodspeed. In his emotional distress Strong began questioning Harper's orthodoxy. Writing to him on the basis of some student notes taken by Strong's daughter on Harper's Saturday lectures at Vassar College, he said he was unwilling, as a parent and trustee of the College "to have the unsuspecting child under the influence of this teaching," and he wrote Mr. Rockefeller that he was sorry to see that apparently Dr. Harper had "departed from the sound faith," and was no longer to be trusted. This particular tack did not mislead Harper's Baptist friends, though it bothered Dr. Harper very much. They were convinced that Mr. Rockefeller's gift would depend to some extent upon the man selected to head the undertaking, and it seemed pretty clear to them that Mr. Rockefeller desired to have Harper in that post, whether Dr. Harper himself really wished it or not. Goodspeed wrote to Harper on January 2, 1889: "Our strong ground of hope is that you have Mr. Rockefeller's ear and confidence as no other man has." Mr. Rockefeller had become very tired over the "pushing and pulling" and he had expressed the hope in a letter of this same date that "you wise men will all see eye to eye" on this matter of Biblical interpretation. On January 15th he wrote to Dr. Harper: "Of late I had rather come to feel that if Chicago could get a college and leave the question of a university until a later date, this would be more likely to be accomplished." He did not decide the issue at once. In fact, as late as April 10, 1889, he was writing to Dr. Strong asking for his views, saying he "favored freedom of expression all around" and assuring him that so far he had made no committals for a university and no immediate prospects of any, though he had, he said, made a pledge of $100,000 to the Baptist Educational Society and was awaiting recommendations from them with respect to disposition of this fund. A committee of the Society did make a report a day or so later. It recommended, among other things, (a) a well-equipped *college*, leaving any desirable further development to the natural outgrowth of time; (b) location of such an institution in the city of Chicago; (c) admission of both sexes on equal terms; (d) a preparatory school "of the highest excellence" to be established; (e) the president and two-thirds of the board of trustees for the institution to be members of the Baptist Church.

The executive board of the Society had already gone on record the previous December as favoring such a plan. On the basis of the committee's report and conferences with Mr. Rockefeller, Dr. Gates secured from Mr. Rockefeller a pledge toward the enterprise—a pledge that was to be kept secret until such time as the Society in its meeting would accept or reject, as the case might be, the plan reported by the committee. Goodspeed has reproduced Dr. Gates's first-hand account of the scene in New York City that May morning in 1889:

After breakfast we stepped out on the street and walked to and fro on the sidewalk in front of his house, No. 4 West Fifty-fourth Street. It was a delicious May morning. It was agreed that the least possible sum on which we could start, the least sum which could or ought to command confidence of permanence, would be $1,000,000. Of this he said he thought he might give as much as $400,000, if it should be absolutely necessary. I explained to him that it would be impossible for the society to raise $600,000 to his $400,000, or even $500,000; that nothing less than $600,000 from him to $400,000 from the denomination gave any promise of success. For success we should have to go before the people of Chicago and the West with the thing *more than half done* at the start. Such a proposition they would not, they could not, allow to fail. Anything less than that would never even get started. It would be doomed to hopelessness and to failure at the outset. "Give $600,000 of the $1,000,000, and everybody would say at the outset: 'This will not, cannot, must not fail; every adverse interest must and will efface itself. The whole denomination, west and east, will rise as one man to do this whether other things are done or not.'" At last, at a certain point near Fifth Avenue, Mr. Rockefeller stopped, faced me, and yielded the point. Never shall I forget the thrill of that moment. I have since then been intimately associated with him. I have seen him give $10,000,000, $30,000,000, $100,000,000, but no gift of his has ever thrilled me as did that first great gift of $600,000, on that May morning after those months of anxious suspense.

After the decisive words, Mr. Rockefeller invited me down to his office to work out the pledge and all the details. I wrote the first drafts of the pledge, and we together worked it over again and again, trying various forms of words until it took the shape in which it stands. The report of the committee in April, defining the institution to be founded, was put by me in the shape of a series of brief, pointed resolutions. Mr. Rockefeller required that I keep his pledge absolutely confidential until the society should have adopted the resolutions without material change. If the society should fail to adopt the resolutions, committing it and the Baptist denomination to the Chicago enterprise as there outlined, *and doing so without any knowledge whatever of his pledge, doing so in advance of any assurance whatever from him, then the pledge was to be returned to him undelivered.*

Dr. Gates went before the meeting of the Society at Boston and the Society adopted the resolutions. The Chicago institution was assured. It was, to be sure, to be a *college*, a Baptist college, though it might grow into a university.

But two important matters had to be taken care of at once—raising the additional $400,000 to meet the conditions of Mr. Rockefeller's offer, and securing a president to lead the new educational venture.

An appeal was sent to the congregations of churches in Chicago and to 1,200 pastors throughout the West for distribution to their people; a systematic plan for personal solicitation was put into operation in the city of Chicago; and by the end of the first sixty days the fund amounted to $200,000, most of it from Baptists—the Baptist contributions at the end of the campaign totaling $233,000. To raise the next $100,000 took another eight months. Marshall Field was prevailed upon to give ten acres of land for a site, and this helped bring gifts from a number of Chicago business men. A Jewish Club of the city, the Standard Club, raised $25,000 for the institution. The total subscription of the year, including all pledges, amounted to $549,000. On September 8, 1890, the trustees of the first University of Chicago changed its name to "The Old University" to clear the way for the new, and on September 10, 1890, the institution was incorporated by the State of Illinois as the University of Chicago.

DRAFTING A PRESIDENT

Meanwhile steps were being taken to make sure that Dr. William Rainey Harper would be the president of the new university or "college." Dr. Harper had not been any too anxious to head the institution, apparently, though most of those in charge of the plans, as already intimated, had thought of him for it from the first. "On one point I must express my opinion strongly," President Northrup had written to Dr. Harper in November, 1888. "You must not hesitate to accept the presidency, which is as certain to come to you as the institution is to exist." Harper had been about ready to "pull out of the whole concern" when Dr. Strong began questioning his orthodoxy. In January, 1889, Morehouse, Gates, and Wallace Buttrick all joined in informing Mr. Rockefeller that "the managers of Yale University have recently made Professor Harper a series of propositions designed to bind him permanently to that institution." They advised him that his acceptance of these proposals would preclude any direct educational work in the Baptist denomination, which they would regard, they said, as "scarcely less than a denominational disaster." Harper's colleagues in Baptist circles made it clear that they were not interested in the presidency themselves and wished only him to be considered. Gates wrote to Harper, when his own name was mentioned in connection with the office (February 17, 1890):

"You know that nothing under heaven could induce me to dream of such a thing except in nightmare and horror." On May 26, 1890, G. S. Goodspeed wrote from New Haven that Dr. Harper seemed more willing to consider the presidency of the new institution than he had understood was the case. "Some experiences which he has had in entering the academic faculty here and observing the working of things have seemed to entirely alter the state of his mind. . . . He should be taken on any terms." And under date of June 4th Dr. Harper informed Thomas W. Goodspeed that "I am much more inclined to consider the Chicago question today than I have been at any time within the past four years." He was being urged from all sides. President Grose of South Dakota wrote: "I feel that it is your mission, not to be escaped, to fill the college presidency. A strong hand is needed to begin wisely there and you have it. Do not argue otherwise. The work of your life is there. I am a prophet in this case." Some argued on the other side. F. K. Sanders, one of Dr. Harper's assistants in the American Institute of Sacred Literature, warned him: "Don't go to Chicago! You will gain money, but you will lose in everything else which you prize. . . . You can develop yourself faster here at Yale in one year than there in five. Don't go!" The Yale group were particularly distressed. Professor George T. Ladd said:

You would in my judgment make the great and irreparable mistake of your life. . . . You "draw" well, undoubtedly. But, my dear fellow, back of you and of all of us here is the one great power that lends to us more effectiveness than we contribute to it. It is "Yale" that draws. While you are in your prime few men will care for a Ph.D. or even a B.A. from your new university, who can manage to get a similar degree from an institution like this.

The situation was undoubtedly difficult for Dr. Harper. The question in his mind, as he told Dr. Gates, was: "Whether or not I can continue my life work as a Biblical specialist, and do this work which the University of Chicago will demand, and if not, whether I am justified in giving up the life work?" When Dr. Gates saw Harper at New Haven on July 10th, Dr. Gates wrote to Mr. Rockefeller, "he was really and strongly reluctant to leave Yale on any terms." Dr. Gates felt, however, that Harper's selection was all but indispensable to the success of the plan. He assured Dr. Harper of "unanimous and enthusiastic action from the trustees as soon as such action will not embarrass you." As he wrote Mr. Rockefeller, Harper's "reputation for scholarship, his evangelistic spirit, his denominational loyalty, his executive talent, his sympathy with popular education, his very extensive personal popularity and large personal following, his extensive acquaintance with good teachers, and power to compel good teaching and inspire hard study . . . the fact that he is a layman, and comes from an institution not Baptist while himself a Baptist"—these and other considerations were such that the trustees cared to consider no other appointment. But Dr. Harper was not only disturbed over the question of his obligation to his lifelong Biblical study. He confided in Dr. Goodspeed that he really did not think it would be possible to begin doing what the denomination would expect, "what the world would expect," with the funds in hand. "There must in some way be an assurance of an additional million."[6] On August 5th Mr. Rockefeller wrote him urging that he accept the presidency:

> I agree with the board of trustees of the Chicago University that you are the man for president, and if you will take it I shall expect great results. I cannot conceive of a position where you can do the world more good; and I confidently expect we will add funds, from time to time, to those already pledged, to place it upon the most favored basis financially. I do not forget that the effort to establish the University grew out of your suggestion to me at Vassar, and I regard you as the father of the institution, starting out under God with such great promise of future usefulness.

In his reply Mr. Harper spoke frankly of his belief in the need of greater resources:

> The denomination, and indeed the whole country, are expecting the University of Chicago to be from the very beginning an institution of the highest rank and character. Already it is talked of in connection with Yale, Harvard, Princeton, Johns Hopkins, the University of Michigan, and Cornell. No one expects that it will be in any respect lower in grade and equipment than the average of the institutions to which I have referred, and yet, with the money pledged, I cannot understand how the expectations can be fulfilled. Naturally we ought to be willing to begin small and grow, but in these days when things are done so rapidly, and with the example of Johns Hopkins before our eyes, it seems a great pity to wait for growth when we might be born full-fledged.

At a conference on August 17, 1890, between Dr. Gates and Dr. Harper (Dr. Gates having previously discussed the matter with Mr. Rockefeller), an arrangement was worked out whereby Dr. Harper could "become president of a University of Chicago and at the same time not practically renounce his chosen life work of Old Testament research, criticism, and instruction." It was as follows:

---

[6] Thomas W. Goodspeed, *The Story of the University of Chicago*, p. 45.

1. The Theological Seminary to be removed to the campus of the University.
2. The Seminary to become an organic part of the University.
3. The Seminary buildings at Morgan Park to be used for a University Academy.
4. Equivalent or better buildings for the Seminary to be erected on the University campus.
5. Instruction in Hebrew and Old Testament criticism to be transferred to University chairs.
6. Dr. Harper to be head professor with salary and full authority over the department.
7. Mr. Rockefeller to give one million dollars as a new, unconditional gift, a part of which would go for aid to the Seminary in carrying out the program.
8. Dr. Harper to visit Mr. Rockefeller and agree to accept the presidency on this program.[7]

At the second meeting of the board of trustees of the new University, held September 18, 1890, Dr. Harper was elected president by a unanimous vote. He did not accept election at once, however, chiefly because he doubted whether he would be regarded as sufficiently orthodox to head a denominational institution. He finally accepted on February 16, 1891.

Yale did not relinquish Dr. Harper willingly. President Timothy Dwight wrote to Dr. Harper on July 18, 1890:

I owe it to myself, however, and to you, to say to you frankly that, in my judgment, after all that has been done for you at Yale, and all that I have myself done, to secure your position, you cannot honorably leave your Yale professorship for this place at Chicago.

And in another letter dated ten days later President Dwight compared Harper's action to that of "a pastor on whose behalf a house or an endowment has, with earnest and continued effort, been secured, and who, when the thing has been accomplished, is called to another parish."

In this case of yours I have been, in a peculiar degree, the beginning, middle, and end of the movement which has secured your position at Yale by a permanent endowment. . . . I would much rather you had never come to Yale at all, than to have had you remain until this effort had been undertaken and completed and then leave for a new position.

[7] Ibid., p. 47.

WILLIAM RAINEY HARPER

What had been thus far the life and work of this college teacher whose services seemed indispensable to the president of Yale, who was almost the only choice of his denominational and educational colleagues to head the projected university, and who, according to the founder himself, was responsible in the first instance for having interested him sufficiently in such a plan that he ultimately provided resources not only for a college but for a graduate university?

William Rainey Harper was born at New Concord, Ohio, on July 24, 1856, in a log cabin still standing on the old National Trails Road just to the south of the Muskingum College grounds. He was of Scotch-Irish ancestry on both sides, and his father was a local merchant and active church worker in the community. He entered the preparatory school of Muskingum College at the age of eight and the College at ten, his biographers tell us, graduating with the degree of Bachelor of Arts at fourteen and delivering the salutatory oration in Hebrew.[8] Following graduation he worked in his father's store, studied Hebrew and other languages, and played the E-flat cornet in the New Concord Silver Cornet Band that toured the State under Harper's management.

To the people of New Concord, Dr. George Vincent says, "Willie Harper seems not to have been an infant prodigy." Contemporaries insist upon his normality. He could read, however, when he was three, and he was but a youngster when he started collecting a library of his own. While he was still clerking in his father's store an opportunity came to him to teach Hebrew; he did it so well that even down into our own times his way of doing it has remained proverbial as a great example of inspired teaching. On the advice of President Paul of Muskingum, whose daughter he afterward married, young Harper went to Yale for graduate study. At New Haven W. D. Whitney and others encouraged him to go on with Hebrew as his field of scholarship, and at the close of his eighteenth year he received the degree of Doctor of Philosophy from Yale, the subject of his thesis being "A Comparative Study of the Prepositions in Latin, Greek, Sanskrit, and Gothic." He went to Tennessee as principal of a secondary school for a year, and then

---

[8] Having been selected by lot, Goodspeed says, from among the three who had taken this language. (*William Rainey Harper*, Chicago, University of Chicago Press, 1928, p. 10.) The data in the present account are mainly from Goodspeed's biography, Professor Paul Shorey's article in the *Dictionary of American Biography* (vol. VIII, pp. 287–292), and Dr. George E. Vincent's paper at the William Rainey Harper Memorial Conference (Robert N. Montgomery, ed., Chicago, University of Chicago Press, 1938).

to Denison University, at Granville, Ohio, where, under E. Benjamin Andrews' direction, he began his college teaching. Appointed in 1879 to teach Hebrew in the Baptist Seminary at Morgan Park, Illinois, he served at first as instructor (because the authorities thought he looked entirely too young for a professor), but immediately established himself and soon acquired a remarkable reputation both locally and nationally. Dr. Vincent says:

With his arrival the seminary began to quiver like a boat fitted with a new and larger motor. His teaching was not a task but an exciting adventure. Then he asked permission to start a summer school of Hebrew. It was a lively success. In a few years the one school had increased to five. Correspondence teaching followed, with printed lessons, textbooks, a special staff. Dr. Harper began to be known throughout the country.[9]

"Chautauqua"—the summer school and conference established on Chautauqua Lake in western New York in the 'seventies—next drew Dr. Harper. In 1883 he was engaged to head the summer school and establish one of his schools of Hebrew there. From Hebrew his teaching went to lecturing of a more general type in Biblical literature and related fields, and he showed that he could hold large audiences on themes not ordinarily regarded as of popular appeal. "No man ever lived," wrote Jesse L. Hurlbut later in his *Story of Chautauqua*, "who could inspire a class with the enthusiasm that he could awaken on the study of Hebrew, could lead his students so far in that language in a six-weeks' course, or could impart such broad and sane views of the Biblical literature."

In 1886 Yale Theological Seminary called him. "Dr. Harper arrived in New Haven with a family of four . . . and an educational and publishing institution," says Dr. Vincent, and further reports that his teaching "aroused ardent enthusiasm. He was soon lecturing to large audiences in New Haven, Boston, New York City, Vassar College."

This, then, had been Harper's career to date. He was thirty-four when he entered upon his duties as president of the "college" at Chicago. He had previously shown talent for organization. He showed it now. Within the short space of twenty-one months, as Goodspeed and others have described it, and before the doors were opened for students, the "college," with seventeen acres as a site, a million dollars and provision for one building, had developed into the University of Chicago, with an enlarged and much improved site, $4,000,000 in resources and provision for ten buildings, with a faculty of 120 teachers, and with an academy, a college, two graduate schools, and a divinity school.

[9] *Proceedings of the William Rainey Harper Memorial Conference*, p. 6.

INITIATING A PROGRAM

In a recent work of fiction dealing with a university not unlike the University of Chicago the young president is made to say: "After I had been picked for this job I read all the biographies of university presidents I could find—Harper and Eliot and Butler and Gilman, and a lot of others. Do you know what I discovered? That everything they had ever succeeded in doing for their respective institutions they had started in their first five years."[10]

President Harper moved fast in the first of his five years, but not until he had made certain that it was a "university" he was to build and not a college. Indeed, Goodspeed insists that Harper's mind was so set on a university that he was unable to function in any other way; that though he had been urged by his friends to have a plan of educational reorganization ready for the meeting of September, 1890, he did not do so. "For the first and only time in his life his prolific mind seemed to be barren of ideas. . . . He had appeared to yield to the necessity of beginning with a college. As a matter of fact, he had never yielded."[11]

Once the million dollars had been added by Mr. Rockefeller for the express purpose of establishing graduate work, however, Dr. Harper had no difficulty in producing a plan. Indeed, it "flashed upon him," to use his own words. This plan of organization was presented to the board of trustees and adopted in their meeting of December, and subsequently made public as *Official Bulletin Number 1*. Five other bulletins followed at short intervals in 1891 and 1892—*The Colleges, The Academies, The Graduate Schools, The Divinity School, The University Extension Division*.

At the time much was made of these plans as something unique in higher education. Goodspeed contrasts "the well matured scheme, the fully elaborated educational plan of Harper at Chicago," with the "tentativeness" of the Johns Hopkins enterprise.[12] Harper himself, however, considered his program "experimental." In the frequently quoted statement, made three years after the opening, in which he attempted to differentiate Chicago from both the historic American college and the Johns Hopkins type, he expressed

[10] James Weber Linn, *Winds Over the Campus*, New York, Bobbs-Merrill Company, 1936, pp. 107–108.

[11] Thomas W. Goodspeed, *The Story of the University of Chicago*, p. 51.

[12] It is possible that Goodspeed interpreted too literally the following passage from Gilman's account of the founding of Johns Hopkins: "Not only did we have no model to be followed; we did not even draw up a scheme or program for the government of ourselves, our associates, and successors. For a long time our proceedings were 'tentative,' and this term was used so often that it became a by-word for merriment." (*The Launching of a University*, p. 49.) Gilman was presumably speaking of organization and administration rather than the educational program in the larger sense. The Hopkins plans were clear and definite. (See pp. 28 ff.)

surprise that there had been no further innovating efforts. "The field for experiment in educational work is as vast as any that may present itself in other departments of activity," he said. "If only those who experiment will be quick to discard that which shows itself to be wrong, the cause of education has nothing to fear from experiment."

THE HARPER PLAN

President Harper's plan provided for organizing the activities of the University under three general divisions—The University Proper, The University Extension Work, The University Publication Work. The University Proper was to include the academy at Morgan Park and any other academies that might develop; the colleges, to consist of the College of Liberal Arts, "in which the curriculum will be arranged with a view to the degree of A.B.," the College of Science, work in which would lead to the B.S., the College of Literature, devoted to languages and literatures, and the College of Practical Arts—also leading to the B.S.; such affiliated colleges as might enter into arrangements with the University; a number of "Schools," the first to be organized to be the Graduate Schools, which would do "all graduate work of non-professional character," and the Divinity School, with others to follow as soon as funds permitted—the Law School, the Medical School, Engineering—civil, mechanical, electrical—the School of Pedagogy, the School of Fine Arts, and the School of Music.

University extension work was to be provided through regular courses of lectures, evening courses, correspondence courses, special courses on the scientific study of the Bible, and library extension.

The activities under "The University Publication Work" were to include:

The printing and publishing of university bulletins, catalogues, and other official documents.

The printing and publishing of special papers, journals, or reviews of a scientific character, prepared and edited by instructors in the various departments of the University.

The printing and publishing of books prepared or edited by instructors in the various departments of the University.

Collecting, by way of exchange, of papers, journals, reviews, and books similar to those published by the University.

Purchase and sale of books for students, professors, and the University libraries.

Much space in this first official bulletin is given over to organizational details—the make-up of the University Council; duties of the University Examiner, the Recorder, the Registrar, the University Extension Secretary, the University Librarian, the University Publisher, the University Steward, as well as the deans of the various colleges and schools and the heads of departments, lecturers, and teachers. The latter group were to be classified as follows: (1) Head Professor; (2) Professor; (3) Professor, non-resident; (4) Associate Professor; (5) Assistant Professor; (6) Instructor; (7) Tutor; (8) Docent; (9) Reader; (10) Lecturer; (11) Fellow; (12) Scholar.

Detailed regulations were made a part of *Official Bulletin No. 1*. Under the regulations "the year shall be divided into four quarters, beginning respectively on the first day of October, January, April, and July," continuing twelve weeks each, and thus leaving a week between the close of one quarter and the beginning of the next. Each quarter was to be divided into two equal terms of six weeks each. Besides the four-quarter plan thus announced, the regulations also gave prominence to a scheme whereby "all courses of instruction shall be classified as Majors and Minors"—a major signifying ten, eleven, or twelve hours of classroom work each week, a minor four, five, or six hours a week.[13]

Unlike Hopkins, Chicago went early into the problem of ranking and marking students. The standing of a student was, under these regulations, to be determined by his "term-grade," from an examination taken immediately at the completion of the course, and from a second examination taken twelve weeks after the date of the first examination.

In other of these early bulletins the colleges are described; requirements for admission are detailed; a distinction is drawn between the *academic college* (covering what are usually known as the freshman and sophomore years) and the *university college* (junior and senior years); and the various "schools" for graduate instruction are listed. Some twenty-one fields of advanced work were contemplated, fourteen of which were to be established immediately (indicated by stars in the following list):

*The School of Philosophy
*The School of Political Economy
 The School of Political Science
*The School of History
*The School of Social Science

[13] In his discussion of the classification of courses in the so-called "unfinished report," prepared a few months before the University opened, President Harper stated that "a subject taken as a major requires eight or ten hours' classroom work or lecture work a week." (Goodspeed, *A History of the University of Chicago*, p. 142.) The major as a term was later defined as either four or five hours per week, depending on the year in which the work came.

*The School of Semitic Languages and Literatures
*The School of Sanskrit, Zend, and Indogermanic Comparative Philology
*The School of Greek Language and Literature
*The School of Latin Language and Literature
*The School of Romance Languages and Literatures
*The School of Germanic Languages and Literatures
*The School of English
*The School of Mathematics and Astronomy
 The School of Physics
*The School of Chemistry
*The School of Biology
 The School of Geology and Mineralogy
 The School of Civil Engineering
 The School of Mechanical Engineering
 The School of Electrical Engineering
 The School of Mining Engineering[14]

It would be easy to criticize adversely at this distance a plan that deals so much with detail. Comparatively few even of the main features strike us as novel or original today, partly, no doubt, because the Chicago experience has accustomed us to take for granted much that seemed new at the time; partly, also, because various parts of the program had been tried elsewhere and were not nearly so revolutionary as they appeared when made part of a comprehensive program.[15] Many of the terms used had already been part of the language of universities, European and American, for years. Some of the more radical departures had precedents: University extension came directly from England; Hopkins had set the example of the University Press some years before; coeducation at the university level was at least a score of years old; and even the use of the summer quarter could be shown to be not unlike the practice of early Eastern colleges and academies.

Ideas Behind the Plan

What is of importance in President Harper's plan as revealed in these bulletins is not the detailed organization, but the purpose behind it—to free students and faculty alike from the handicaps of the traditional college and

[14] University of Chicago, "Graduate Schools of the University," *Official Bulletin No. 4*, Chicago, 1892.

[15] An illustration of the reputation Chicago had in the early days is afforded in the following passage from an article by E. E. Slosson: "Beginning in 1891 [William Rainey Harper] issued a series of revolutionary manifestoes which burst like bombs in the educational world. The West received them with amazement; the East with amusement. But the amazement soon changed into admiration, the amusement into trepidation. For the new projects were not merely broad; they were iconoclastic. . . .

"The summer quarter was the most radical and most successful of the innovations. It was not merely

enable them to live and work in an atmosphere of scholarship and research. Dr. Harper could be on occasion a very severe critic of the colleges. In a discussion of "waste in higher education" he once wrote:

The American college system has actually murdered hundreds of men who while in its service have felt that something more must be done than the work of the classroom, and who, because of this feeling, have died from overwork. It has actually destroyed the intellectual growth of thousands of strong and able men.[16]

President Harper believed that his plan would secure concentration on the part of students, permit admission at several times during the year, break up the conventional method of passing all students through the same courses, raise standards of work, and enable men to utilize the fourth quarter for additional intellectual work, for employment, or to make up time lost in illness. But over and above these practical considerations, Dr. Harper felt that the plan would furnish better opportunities for original research and investigation; secure a greater degree of intimacy between instructors and students; give members of the instructional staff longer vacation periods with pay; make it possible for university faculty and students to utilize the resources of other institutions in America and Europe; and "encourage an independent feeling on the part of all men who share the advantages of the University." The comparatively light schedule for each instructor—eight or ten hours a week—was designed to allow ample time and energy for independent study and research.

That part of the Harper plan calling for "affiliation" with neighboring colleges was also in the direction of establishing the University as a place for advanced work. Of course, in attempting this the University was setting out on what has proved to be one of the most difficult tasks in American higher education. Just as President Gilman at Johns Hopkins had pointed to the existing City College, girls' high schools, and St. John's as good and sufficient reasons why the new Johns Hopkins should do *university* and not *collegiate* work, so President Harper put on record in *Official Bulletin No. 2* (April, 1891) the plan for "entering into affiliation with colleges situated at different points," and the hope that "the academic college work of the University will be accomplished in large measure through its affiliated

the extension of the session for the better utilization of the plant or the shortening of the college course. Its most marked effect was to loosen up the college system and give it a flexibility that enabled it to adapt itself to varying conditions as never before." (*Independent*, January 6, 1910.)

[16] William Rainey Harper, *The Trend in Higher Education*, Chicago, University of Chicago Press, 1905, p. 107.

colleges," to the end that the University of Chicago might be permitted "to devote its energies mainly to the University Colleges and to strictly University work."

President Harper submitted his plan to many educational leaders. Among those who realized clearly that a university, rather than a college, was being set up rapidly in Chicago was Dr. Augustus H. Strong. When asked by President Harper to comment on the plan of organization sent him late in 1890, Dr. Strong admitted that he was greatly impressed, though he was sure that "to carry it out fully would require no less money than I wished for a university in the city of New York." He questioned the practicability of the four-quarter plan, but said he should be interested in seeing it tried. He hesitated to approve the correspondence courses. He was much disturbed at the absence of any provision for making sure of the theological orthodoxy and religious character of the teachers in the institution: "I do not know why Baptists should concern themselves about education at all, unless they aim to establish institutions which fill a totally different place from those founded on a secular basis by individuals or by the State." And he was quite definite in his opinion that it was most unwise to try to carry on both college and graduate work:

> You turn back the wheels of time and ignore the lessons of the past by attempting to combine in one institution both postgraduate and academical work. Johns Hopkins has seen that this is a mistake. The best work cannot be done by teachers who teach both [under] graduates and postgraduates together—nor is the effect upon students good of mixing both classes in one institution.

But Dr. Strong was willing to admit freely that the whole plan was an imposing one, particularly suited to Dr. Harper's abilities. "I doubt," he said, "whether any one but yourself could carry it out. . . . If it succeeds, it will unquestionably attract the widest attention both at home and abroad."[17]

DEVELOPMENT OF GRADUATE WORK

President Harper's carefully detailed plan of organization was intended, among other things, to strengthen the more advanced work of the University, particularly at the upper collegiate and graduate education levels. The trend towards graduate work was further stimulated by aid from an unexpected source—the Ogden Fund.

[17] Letter of Augustus H. Strong to W. R. Harper, December 23, 1890 (in the Harper correspondence at the University of Chicago).

William B. Ogden had been for many years a trustee of the first University of Chicago. After his death the executors of his estate, Andrew H. Green and Mrs. Ogden, entered into negotiations with President Harper with a view to establishing a graduate school of science. The agreement reached was that seventy per cent of the moneys to be devoted to benevolences under the terms of Mr. Ogden's will should go to the University of Chicago as endowment for the Ogden Graduate School of Science, and Dr. Goodspeed is authority for the statement that eventually nearly $600,000 was thereby added to the funds of the University.

Late in 1891 Mr. Rockefeller gave another million dollars "to remain forever a further endowment for the University, the income to be used only for the current expenses." In February, 1892, Sydney A. Kent offered to provide a chemical laboratory, and in April of the same year Marshall Field agreed to give $100,000 to the new university on condition that a million dollars be secured in sixty days—later extended to ninety days. Slightly more than the million was in hand on July 9, 1892, and a group of twenty local business men had pledged themselves pro rata to make good any deficiency up to a hundred thousand dollars.

It is significant of the emphasis upon educational aims and objectives that T. W. Goodspeed closes his discussion of the physical expansion of the University, made possible by this 1892 gift, with the comment: "This fund provided the material expansion corresponding to the educational enlargement made possible by the Rockefeller endowment and the Ogden designation."[18]

SECURING A FACULTY

In the meantime, President Harper had gone ahead on the task of securing a faculty. The fundamental significance of the human factor in university education—that "it is men and nothing but men that make education"—was accepted from the first in Chicago. "If the first faculty of the University of Chicago had met in a tent, this would still have been a great university," said the present head of the institution when he entered office.[19] The one function Dr. Harper would not delegate to others was the selection and nomination of new members of the staff.

President Harper and the trustees had decided against the policy of selecting a few younger instructors and allowing the work in the various depart-

---

[18] Thomas W. Goodspeed, *The Story of the University of Chicago*, p. 75.

[19] Robert Maynard Hutchins, *Inaugural Address*, November 19, 1929, Chicago, University of Chicago Press, p. 13.

ments to develop "under the domination of a single spirit." Instead, as Dr. Harper later described in his report, they were determined "to bring together the largest possible number of men who had already shown their strength in their several departments, each of whom, representing a different training and a different set of ideas, would contribute much to the ultimate constitution of the University."[20]

But getting a faculty on these conditions proved to be exceedingly difficult. As late as December 26, 1891, President Harper wrote that he was "completely discouraged," that the situation was growing darker every day. "We have not a head professor after nine months of constant work. Not one of the men that we want can be moved from a good position at the salary of six thousand dollars. I am in despair."[21] In spite of the comparatively high salaries offered—for the amount just indicated was later increased to seven thousand—"many noted scholars were reluctant," Dr. Goodspeed says, "to leave assured positions for what, in spite of President Harper's confidence and optimism, might prove to be a dream university." For example, Professor Herbert B. Adams, of Johns Hopkins, when invited for the history department, replied that his professional and scientific interests lay in the Johns Hopkins University, and later, when importuned still further, he replied (letter of December, 1891), "I like you and Chicago and all that your new combination represents, but I have chosen Babylonian captivity rather than an Egyptian alliance."

Dean Marion Talbot, describing the efforts of President Harper as he "scoured the academic world for great scholars who would dare exchange comfortable and safe positions for the hazards and excitement of a new undertaking," tells of the experience with Professor George Herbert Palmer, of Harvard, whom President Harper wanted to head his new Department of Philosophy, and his wife, Alice Freeman Palmer, formerly president of Wellesley College, who was sought as professor of history and dean of women in the Graduate School and College. President Harper's efforts to secure Professor Palmer on any regular basis were unsuccessful, but Mrs. Palmer agreed to give part-time service, and this arrangement—not unlike the plan at Hopkins in Gilman's time—prevailed for three years.[22]

It was the discovery that Clark University, Worcester, Massachusetts, established under G. Stanley Hall only a short while before to do exclusively graduate work, had faculty members who were dissatisfied that gave Dr.

[20] University of Chicago, *President's Report*, 1892–1902, p. xvii.
[21] Thomas W. Goodspeed, *A History of the University of Chicago*, p. 206.
[22] Marion Talbot, *More Than Lore*, Chicago, University of Chicago Press, 1936, pp. 2–4.

Harper his first significant opening. From the Clark science group Harper was able to secure three greatly needed "head professors," as well as a number of other highly qualified teachers and research workers of varying academic rank. Whatever one may think of the crisis at Clark and the effects on the Worcester institution, from the Chicago point of view it was heaven-sent. "It was a severe blow to us then," Dr. Hall himself wrote years later, "but the men were all ideally devoted to science and have been given larger opportunities than they would have had here" [at Worcester]. This migration from Clark provided the new university with a group of the best-equipped men to be had anywhere in America, already selected and trained to do, in graduate work especially, the very things Harper wanted the University of Chicago to undertake.

The faculty as finally selected for the opening year came from all sections of the United States and from several foreign countries. Eight had held positions as presidents of colleges and universities.[23] A contemporary French visitor, marveling at the rapid growth of the new university, told his countrymen how Dr. Harper summoned faculty members from everywhere: "He took a physician here, a history teacher there; he brought chemists and theologians from afar."[24]

A significant departure in the Chicago situation was the recognition of women both as faculty members and students. Women had had no recognized status in the early Hopkins and Clark experience, though at Hopkins an individual like Christine Ladd might be informally accepted and at Clark President Hall had favored inclusion of women students. One of the first undertakings of the Association of Collegiate Alumnae, organized in 1882 (later the American Association of University Women), was a study of the possibilities of graduate work for women; hitherto, in Dean Talbot's words, it had been "a distinctly masculine procession that was advancing into the field of research and scholarship." At Chicago women were appointed to the faculty and awarded graduate fellowships from the start. The first number of the *Quarterly Calendar* of the University, June, 1892, listed, as members of the staff of the new university, not only "Alice Freeman Palmer, Ph.D., Litt.D., Professor of History and Acting Dean (of Women) in the Graduate School of the University Colleges," but also "Julia E. Bulkley, Associate Professor of Pedagogy and Dean (of Women) in the Academic College."

---

[23] Dean Talbot remarks that in 1936 eighteen of this original faculty were still connected with the University of Chicago, four of them in active service. (*More Than Lore*, p. 14.)

[24] Henri Moissan, *L'Université de Chicago*, Paris, Firmin-Didot et cie., 1897.

The same announcement carried the names of six women who were to be recipients of fellowships.

The task of securing faculty seemed endless. One appointment led to another—often for balancing or offsetting the views of the first appointee. In June, 1892, the secretary of the University announced that the University by that time had "organized its faculties in a somewhat complete way," with sixty instructors in all departments and ten or twelve names to be added. He thought he was giving authentic information, he afterwards said, but he was really "only announcing the number for whom financial provision had been made." As it turned out, it was not "ten or twelve," but sixty that were added before fall, so that when the University opened, its staff included 120 persons—more faculty members than Johns Hopkins had students in its first years.

In this faculty were thirteen head professors, one of whom, Mr. Michelson, spent the year abroad. "There were twenty-one professors—one emeritus and three non-resident." C. R. Van Hise, later president of the University of Wisconsin, was a non-resident professor of geology. Of associate professors there were sixteen and of assistant professors twenty-seven. There were fifteen instructors, nine tutors, four assistants, seven readers, and nine docents. In addition there were seven university extension lecturers. There were sixty-one fellows, some of whom gave more or less instruction.[25]

Four notable appointments made in February, 1892, were those of Hermann Eduard von Holst as head professor of history; Richard Green Moulton as university extension professor of English literature; Emil G. Hirsch as professor of rabbinical literature and philosophy; and Ezekiel G. Robinson as professor of apologetics. Professor von Holst was one of the distinguished European scholars Dr. G. Stanley Hall had sought to bring to Clark University several years before, and indeed Professor von Holst had indicated his willingness to come to America at that time, but Dr. Hall's plans had gone awry. Professor Moulton, a pioneer in university extension in England, had met President Harper in Washington, D. C., and yielded to Harper's urgency to the extent of agreeing to spend a year at Chicago—a year that "became a life engagement."

Another who early joined the staff was Thomas C. Chamberlain, "fresh from a five-year job of reorganizing the University of Wisconsin." He came as head of the Department of Geology and brought with him his professor of geology, Rollin D. Salisbury. An appointment that brought distinction

---

[25] Thomas W. Goodspeed, *A History of the University of Chicago,* p. 247.

to the University over the years was that of Charles O. Whitman as head professor of biology. Professor Whitman had been one of the Clark University group. His coming and that of some of his Clark colleagues undoubtedly helped to give the new university a rather unexpected scientific emphasis, especially in conjunction with the timely gift of the Ogden Fund.[26]

The group in mathematics at the new university was conspicuous, too. "Almost over night," says Professor Birkhoff of Harvard in a recent article, "the great University of Chicago sprang into existence in 1892, with a mathematical department made up of Eliakim Hastings Moore, Oskar Bolza and Heinrich Maschke from Germany, and others. . . . They formed a notable and inspiring group which will ever be remembered in our mathematical annals."[27]

By 1904 Nott William Flint was able to describe the "permanent organization" of Departments at the University as follows:

Philosophy, John Dewey; Political Economy, James Laurence Laughlin; Political Science, Harry Pratt Judson; History, Hermann Eduard von Holst, 1892–1900, John Franklin Jameson, 1901; Sociology, Albion Woodbury Small; Semitic Languages and Literatures, William Rainey Harper; Biblical and Patristic Greek, Ernest Dewitt Burton; Greek Language and Literature, Paul Shorey; Latin Language and Literature, William Gardner Hale; Romance Languages and Literatures, William Ireland Knapp, 1892–93; English Language and Literature, John Matthews Manly; Mathematics, Eliakim Hastings Moore; Physics, Albert Abraham Michelson; Chemistry, John Ulric Nef; Geology, Thomas Chrowder Chamberlin; Biology, Charles Otis Whitman; Zoology, Charles Otis Whitman; Anatomy, Lewellys Franklin Barker; Physiology, Jacques Loeb, 1900–1903; Neurology, Henry Herbert Donaldson; Palaeontology, Samuel Wendell Williston; Botany, John Merle Coulter; Pathology and Bacteriology, Ludvig Hektoen.[28]

MEETING CONTEMPORARY NEEDS

As with Johns Hopkins, one of the elements that accounted for the success

[26] "The University of Chicago . . . which has leaped into existence with a Minerva-like completeness, owing in no small part its first impulse to higher creative work in science to the chief trustee of the Ogden Fund, our fellow-townsman, Andrew H. Green, and still more closely affiliated to us by the fact that so many of the leading members of its faculty honored us by doing three years of their best work here, and for which we still cherish a little of the feeling of a poor but proud and noble mother for her great son." (G. Stanley Hall, Decennial address at Clark University, Decennial Celebration, p. 45.)

[27] George D. Birkhoff, "Fifty Years of American Mathematics," *Science*, 88:463–467, November 18, 1938.

[28] Nott William Flint, *The University of Chicago: A Sketch*, Chicago, University of Chicago Press, 1904.

at Chicago was the determination to face squarely the needs of the age and attempt to meet these needs regardless of what this might mean in abandonment of conventional policy and practice. "If the proposal were simply to go to Chicago and organize another university just like others already in existence," Dr. Harper said to Professor Tufts in December, 1890, "I would not think of it for a moment. It is the opportunity to do something new and different which appeals to me."[29] Harper felt as strongly as Gilman the obligation to bring higher education more into accord with the demands of the age. "The most marked characteristic in the development of university life in the last twenty-five years," he said at the winter convocation of 1895, "has been the adaptation of its methods and training to the practical problems of the age in which we live." Thoroughly aware of the risks involved in a narrow conception of the "practical," and determined not to be rushed into a program of dissociated technological instruction, President Harper nevertheless insisted that all the fields opened up by modern civilization should be represented systematically in higher education. "The University will be derelict in the performance of its duty if it does not enter these fields; for unless it does enter them, it will fail to produce the kind of man which is demanded for them. The times are asking not merely for men to harness electricity and sound, but for men to guide us in complex economic and social duties. Scientific laboratories in the new learning have been fitted to meet the needs of the age, and now scientific guidance and investigation of great economic and social matters of everyday importance are the crying needs." He reminded his hearers that in the original Chicago plan there were two provisions that were particularly intended to meet these needs—the proposed College of Practical Arts, and the "very broad and full" organization of the departments of History, Political Science, Political Economy, and Sociology, which by this time had no less than twenty-four full-time faculty members. When Edwin E. Slosson made his visit to the University some years later, in 1909, he was still impressed with the fact that the innovations made possible by President Harper, while varying in character and effectiveness, seemed for the most part to have had a common aim—"the breaking down of the barriers between the life of the university and the life outside, barriers which six centuries of scholasticism had erected, buttressed, and adorned."[30]

Research and investigation, directly provided for in the Constitution of the University, were obligatory upon all, but President Harper's statement

[29] Quoted in Thomas W. Goodspeed, *A History of the University of Chicago*, pp. 131–132.
[30] *The Independent*, January 6, 1910, p. 22.

at the winter convocation of 1895 indicates that what he had in mind was something much more significant than research of the conventional type:

It is not enough that instructors in a university should merely do the class and lecture work assigned them. This is important, but the University will in no sense deserve the name, if time and labor are not also expended in the work of producing that which will directly or indirectly influence thought and life outside the University. In other words, the responsibilities of the instructors are by no means limited to the work which is done in the classroom. The University, including every member of the University, owes to the world at large a duty which cannot be discharged in the ordinary classroom exercise. The true university is the center of thought on every problem connected with human life and work, and the first obligation resting upon the individual members which compose it is that of research and investigation.[31]

Indeed, Dr. Harper accepted as his definition of a "university of today" one that included "an agency recognized by the people for resolving the problems of civilization which present themselves in the development of civilization"; a place where "definite and distinct effort" is put forth to guide the people in the decision of questions which from time to time confront them—"with the sole purpose of discovering truth, whatever bearing that discovery may have upon other supposed truth. This requires men of the greatest genius, equipment of the highest order, and absolute freedom from interference of any kind, civic or ecclesiastical. . . . The University touches life, every phase of life, at every point."[32]

Replying to the criticism leveled at the University in some quarters during the first years because it did not promptly institute "technological departments," President Harper said:

It seemed upon the whole wise to devote the entire energy of the institution in scientific lines to departments of pure science, with the purpose of establishing these upon a strong foundation. This work being finished, there would be ample opportunity for the other work, and the other work would be all the stronger when it came, because of the earlier and more stable foundation of pure science.[33]

In an environment like Chicago, he felt, where "practical" needs were so obvious they would almost surely be met, there was great danger that pure

---

[31] Statement from the *Annual Register of the University of Chicago*, quoted by President Harper in his address at the winter convocation, 1895. (*Quarterly*, May, 1895, p. 11.)

[32] William Rainey Harper, *The Trend in Higher Education*, pp. 5, 8.

[33] University of Chicago, *President's Report*, 1892–1902, p. xviii.

science might be left without provision. But "active ambition for human service," "knowledge for general use" was the ideal. President Harper sought to imbue his fellow workers with the idea that scholarship should be promoted as zealously as though it were an end unto itself, but that "the final appraisal of scholarship should be, not its prestige with scholars, but its value to human life," and that the university should not be a retreat from the world so much as "a base of operations in the world."[34]

The re-facing of the educational task involved in President Harper's efforts is clearly one of the things that gave vitality to the new University of Chicago, just as it normally does to any educational enterprise. It had a stimulating effect on all engaged in it. "The original faculty who began so hopefully in 1892," said President Harry Pratt Judson some years later, "owed a large part of their enthusiasm doubtless to the fact that they were looking into the future; they were less concerned with what was than with what they could create."

STUDENTS, FACULTY, ADMINISTRATION

Getting a picture of what happened at the University of Chicago in the early years is much more difficult, despite an apparent wealth of material on the subject, than is the case with Johns Hopkins and Clark, largely because of the rapid growth of numbers and the magnitude and complexity of the Chicago enterprise. Figures already given indicate that the faculty in the first year was larger than the entire student body at the other two places. In 1887 Dr. Harper had ventured to predict that, if a university were established at Chicago, "in ten years such a university would have more students, if rightly conducted, than Yale or Harvard has today." At that time Harvard had 1,688 students in all departments, Yale 1,245. Chicago by its fourth year already had 1,815 students, and the Harper prediction could safely have been, as it happened, "nearly three times as many students as Harvard" and "nearly four times as many as Yale." In its third year of operation the University of Chicago had 534 graduate students, as compared with fewer than a hundred at Hopkins for the corresponding year and eighty at Clark. Three or four years later the number of graduate students at Chicago had passed the thousand mark.

It would have been miraculous if under these circumstances the informality and intimate personal relationships that characterized faculty, student, and administration at Baltimore and Worcester had likewise prevailed

[34] Albion W. Small, in *The Biblical World*, March, 1906, pp. 217–218.

at Chicago. That there was an unusually fine spirit, however, is the testimony of most of those who were part of the University at this period. Dean Marion Talbot, reminiscing many years later, records that in the constant stream of faculty callers at the President's office each was somehow made to feel that his relation to his chief was personal, nor merely official. This was true of students also, Miss Talbot says:

> Individual conferences and consultation with groups tended to build up an extraordinary sense of unity. The gatherings of prospective candidates for advanced degrees for a matutinal breakfast at his house on Convocation Day, the student councils whose meetings and policies interested him greatly, the congregation whose membership included not only Faculty but Doctors of the University, the Convocation receptions, where a special welcome was given to the relatives and friends of the graduating students—these and many other ways to whose success Mrs. Harper contributed generously, built up a spirit which was quite unique. It certainly struck my mother that way, for she recalled how my brother, up to the time of his graduation from Harvard College, had never met President Eliot. . . . It was amply shown that kindness and friendliness, and even a certain amount of informality, were not inconsistent with conventional standards of social intercourse.[35]

What is here described, desirable though it must have been, and a refreshing change from the academic stiffness of the day, was hardly the same as the informal living and working together on the part of faculty and students that are everywhere testified to in the case of Johns Hopkins and Clark. Whatever there was of this in the new University of Chicago—and there seems to have been some—must have come from the fact that, though the University was large, even from the start, the graduate groups in the many departments were small, and in charge of some of these departments were teachers and research workers, particularly the distinguished group acquired from Clark, who were already acquainted from their previous experience with the possibilities of individual work and a closer student-teacher relationship at the graduate level. Systematic effort was made, as in the formation of the Quadrangle Club, to break down barriers and encourage personal and intellectual companionship, but this must have been a very difficult task.

The seminars organized in the various departments, with "academic college and University college seminars distinct in the same department," had as their purpose, Dr. Harper explained in the statement intended to be used

---

[35] Marion Talbot, *More Than Lore*, p. 36.

as part of his first annual report, "to promote advanced study and individual research, and to bring together instructors and students."

GRADUATE EDUCATION AND RESEARCH

Insistence upon the research function was accompanied by some practical measures that again show how far Chicago was determined to go in changing teaching conditions from those of the traditional American college.[36] Research was to be a first requirement, not a rather remote extra possibility:

If the instructor is loaded down with lectures, he will have neither time nor strength to pursue his investigations. Freedom from care, time for work, and liberty of thought are prime requisites in all such work. . . . It is expected that professors and other instructors will, at intervals, be excused entirely for a period from lecture work, in order that they may thus be able to give their entire time to the work of investigation. . . . In other words, it is proposed in this institution to make the work of investigation primary, the work of giving instruction secondary.[37]

Emphasis upon research was intensified by the definite provision—even more specific than a similar provision at Clark—that "promotion of younger men in the departments will depend more largely upon the results of their work as investigators than upon the efficiency of their teaching, although the latter will by no means be overlooked." This was based, of course, on the same philosophy with regard to the relation of research and teaching held by Gilman and Hall—that "it is only the man who has made investigation who may teach others to investigate. Without this spirit in the instructor, and without his example, students will never be led to undertake the work."

To the end Dr. Harper was convinced that it was in the graduate schools of the University that his ideals in research and all that they implied for advanced university work were realized. At the June Convocation of 1903 he was able to say that "nearly every member of every department in the University is today engaged in investigative work in which effort is being put forth to make new contributions toward the better understanding of the subject studied."[38] He reported at this time on sixty-five pieces of research that were under way by faculty members and graduate students in nine departments of the University, indicating that this was but a fraction of the total and that he planned to present later the work done in other de-

[36] As at Harvard, for example. See footnote on p. 74.

[37] President Harper's incomplete report, as given in Goodspeed, *The Story of the University of Chicago,* pp. 60–61.

[38] *University Record,* July, 1903, p. 45.

partments. In the years that followed, these reports of investigations as they appeared in the annual presidential reports came to fill between twenty and thirty closely printed pages and covered twenty-five and more departments. Says Goodspeed:

> High honors came to many of the professors for their achievements in the advancement of knowledge. Some of them were employed for a part of their time to conduct special investigations for the Carnegie Institution. Some received great prizes for notable achievements in science. Some were called on by foreign nations for assistance in arranging their fiscal systems. Some were called to Berlin and Paris for courses of lectures in the German and French universities. In the annual call made on the universities of this country for heads or resident professors at the American Schools of Rome, Athens, and Jerusalem, professors of the Graduate Schools were frequently chosen.[39]

FREEDOM OF TEACHING

With respect to freedom of teaching and learning the new university took a decided stand. When the founder, John D. Rockefeller, was consulted about the opening ceremonies he instructed Dr. Gates, his representative, to say that "while he is, of course, closely interested in the conduct of the institution, he has refrained from making suggestions and would prefer in general not to take an active part in the counsels of the management. He prefers to rest the whole weight of the management on the shoulders of the proper officers."

Apparently there had been a superior tradition, even in the old University of Chicago, on this important matter of freedom of teaching. Though founded by Baptists and operating under a provision that required the president of the institution and a majority of the trustees to be Baptists, the old University nevertheless had made it a rule from Stephen Douglas's time down that "no religious test or particular religious profession shall ever be held as a requisite for admission to any department of the University, or for election to any professorship or other place of honor or emolument in it, but the same shall be open alike to persons of any religious faith or profession."[40]

President Harper was determined to maintain the policy of independence of teaching and learning. "The principle of complete freedom of speech on all subjects," he said, "has been regarded as fundamental in the University of Chicago. No donor has any right, before God or man, to interfere with the

[39] Thomas W. Goodspeed, *A History of the University of Chicago*, p. 372.
[40] Ibid., p. 18.

teaching of officers appointed to give instruction in a university." And he went on to say, as bluntly as he knew how:

When for any reason, in a university or private foundation, or in a university supported by public money, administration of the institution or the instruction in any of its departments is changed by an influence from without; when an effort is made to dislodge an officer or a professor because the political sentiment or the religious sentiment of the majority has undergone a change, at that moment the institution has ceased to be a university, and it cannot again take its place in the rank of universities so long as there continues to any appreciable extent the factor of coercion. Neither an individual, nor the state, nor the church, has the right to interfere with the search for truth, or with its promulgation when found. Individuals, or the state, or the church, may found schools for propagating certain special kinds of instruction, but such schools are not universities, and may not be so denominated. . . .

In order to be specific, and in order not to be misunderstood, I wish to say again that no donor of funds to the university—and I include in the number of donors the founder of the University, Mr. Rockefeller—has ever by a single word or act indicated his dissatisfaction with the instruction given to students in the University or with the public expression of opinion made by an officer of the University.[41]

The hazards involved in assembling a faculty made up of persons of widely varying views and sometimes explosive tendencies and then allowing them this freedom of thought and expression were fully recognized. One appointee, upon learning of the selection of a colleague with whose views he differed radically, said: "If it is true that —— is to be on the faculty, plans ought to be made at once for a bomb-proof wall between the departments we shall occupy. The best work I have done in [my field] has been on the thesis that the more —— writes on [this subject] the more conclusively he proves that he is thirty years behind the times." Yet, says Goodspeed, "these two professors lived and labored together in perfect amity and thorough cooperation." Men as different in their social outlook as J. Laurence Laughlin and Thorstein Veblen worked together at Chicago; indeed, at Laughlin's death in 1933 a writer in the *Journal of Political Economy* mentioned as an outstanding achievement on Laughlin's part the fact that he had brought Veblen to Chicago.[42]

That freedom in this form would work was not at all certain at first. "It

[41] University of Chicago, *President's Report*, 1892–1902, p. xxiii.

[42] Joseph Dorfman, *Thorstein Veblen and His America*, p. 517. See also John U. Nef, "James Laurence Laughlin (1850–1933)," *Journal of Political Economy*, vol. 42, no. 1, February, 1934, p. 2.

was an open question whether with so large a number of eminent men, each maintaining his own ideas, there could be secured even in a long time that unity of spirit without which an institution could not prosper." These doubts seemed very real throughout the first year, President Harper relates, but "during the middle of the second year certain events occurred which led up to the birth, as it were, of the spirit of unity which had not been hoped for. The Saturday morning on which this new spirit first manifested itself in its fullness may well be regarded as the date of the spiritual birth of the institution."[43]

Abuses of the privilege of freedom of teaching would undoubtedly occur, Dr. Harper foresaw, but he felt that in such cases it was proper and right that the University itself should suffer, since these were the direct and inevitable consequence of lack of foresight and wisdom in the original appointments. In any event, abuse of the privilege was no justification for curtailment of it:

> Freedom of expression must be given the members of a university faculty, even though it be abused, for, as has been said, the abuse of it is not so great an evil as the restriction of such liberty. . . .
> A professor is guilty of an abuse of his privileges who promulgates as truth ideas or opinions which have not been tested scientifically by his colleagues in the same department of research or investigation. . . . The University is no place for partisanship. From the teacher's desk should emanate the discussion of principles, the judicial statements of arguments from various points of view, and not the one-sided representations of a partisan character.[44]

Interesting in this connection is the way in which the new University managed to keep research going in religious as well as in other fields. The persistence of the original religious interest and mingling of two types of research are illustrated by the following title and contents of a volume of studies published by the University of Chicago Press in 1903:

Investigations representing the departments.
Chicago, University of Chicago Press, 1903.
Part 1, Systematic Theology, church history, practical theology.
Part 2, Philosophy, education.

CONTENTS

PART 1. Johnson, F. *Have We the Likeness of Christ?* Henderson, C. R. *Practical Sociology in the Service of Social Ethics.* Anderson, G. *The Elements of Chrysostum's Power*

---

[43] University of Chicago, *President's Report*, 1892–1902, pp. xviii–xix.

[44] Ibid., p. xxiii.

as a Preacher. Smith, G. B. *Practical Theology: A Neglected Field in Theological Education.*
PART 2. Tufts, J. H. *On the Genesis of the Aesthetic Categories.* Angell, J. R. *A Preliminary Study of the Significance of Partial Tones in the Localization of Sound.* Moore, A. W. *Existence, Meaning, and Reliability in Locke's Essay and his Present Epistemology.* Angell, J. R. *The Relations of Structural and Functional Psychology to Philosophy.* Mead, G. H. *The Definition of the Psychical.* Dewey, J. *The Logical Conditions of a Scientific Treatment of Morality.* Young, E. F. *Scientific Method in Education.*

UNIVERSITY OF CHICAGO PRESS

Publication activities at the University of Chicago were initiated specifically to encourage research. Under President Harper's leadership Chicago made more of this than either Hopkins or Clark had done. From the beginning it was one of the five major divisions of the University. Here two of the president's purposes coincided—that of making the work of the research staff known to other workers through scientific journals, books, and monographs, and that of extension, i.e., extending the benefits of college and university instruction wherever feasible to the public at large.

"An essential element is the opportunity of publishing results obtained in investigations," Dr. Harper wrote in one of the sections of his incomplete report prepared a few months before the University opened. "To this end it is provided that in each department there shall be published either a journal or a series of separate studies which shall in each department embody the results of the work of the instructors in that department."

The *Journal of Political Economy* was the first of these periodicals. It was followed almost immediately by the *Journal of Geology*, and shortly after by the *Biblical World*, the *American Journal of Semitic Languages and Literatures* (formerly *Hebraica*) and the *University Extension World*—all before the close of the first year of the University's life. Development of later journals is summarized as follows by Thomas W. Goodspeed in his shorter history:

In 1895 came the *Astrophysical Journal* and the *American Journal of Sociology*. In 1896 the *Botanical Gazette* and the *School Review* appeared and the *University Record* succeeded the *Quarterly Calendar*. At the beginning of 1897 the *American Journal of Theology* was started, later combining with the *Biblical World* to form the *Journal of Religion*. After 1897 no new journals were added to the list for four years. Then a new period of activity began. The Chicago Institute, which became the School of Education of the University of Chicago in 1901, brought with it a journal which after two changes of name became the *Elementary School Journal.* In 1903 *Modern Philology* appeared, in 1906, *Classical Philology.*[45]

GRADUATE WORK AND HEAVY ENROLLMENTS

By implication at least the question has already been raised as to the effect of rapid growth in student enrollments on the purposes for which the University of Chicago was created under Harper's leadership. Wherever, as in the case of Chicago, there is a spectacular expansion in enrollments and physical plant, the temptation is to make a quantitative statement that will delight those who measure success primarily in size. One could point out, for example, that the 744 students in all departments of 1892 had increased to 13,357 by 1923; that the number of graduate students alone went from 166 in 1892 to 1,120 in 1905 and over 2,300 in 1915—exclusive of divinity and law; that the faculty increased six-fold in thirty years; that nearly a thousand separate courses were offered in the graduate school, many of them research courses; that the degrees granted each year in all departments of the University rose from thirty-one in 1893 to 1,456 in 1924, and that of the more than fifteen hundred men and women who received doctor's degrees in the first thirty years, approximately a thousand were at the close of that period holding positions in colleges and universities throughout the country.

But, as the University authorities said when they presented these and other statistics in 1925,[46] "the best measurement of the value of a university is not to be made by the number of its students or its schools"; it is, rather, in the "quality of an institution's work and its contributions to knowledge and educational training and practice." One interesting fact that suggests something more important than numbers is that of the four Americans who won Nobel prizes in science in the first quarter century of Nobel awards, three were members of the faculty of the University of Chicago. Other claims that have been put forth in behalf of the University on the qualitative side, especially for the first fifteen or twenty years, include achievements such as are represented in the establishment of the University of Chicago Press; Michelson's researches in stellar measurement and the velocity of light; Small's work in organizing the study of sociology.

A summary of the graduate and research accomplishments of the first years of the University is given in the 1925 publication already cited:

The University's foundation opened an epoch in American education

[45] Thomas W. Goodspeed, *The Story of the University of Chicago*, pp. 142–143.
[46] *The University of Chicago: Its Future*, Chicago, University of Chicago Press, 1925, pp. 5–6.

largely because of the fresh emphasis which it laid upon research, the eminent scholars whom it called into its service, and the unparalleled opportunities for advanced work which it offered to college graduates ambitious to become scholars and teachers.

The aim of the Graduate Schools is twofold—first, research for the sake of the discoveries which will thus be made, and second, the education of students in methods of research, with a view to their becoming discoverers themselves and teachers who will train others to follow in their footsteps.

It is the spirit of research, the eager and organized effort to enlarge the area of human knowledge, to replace guesses by certainties, to open new areas of knowledge, to organize data and extract from them new knowledge, that is the most characteristic work of the modern university. We shall still try to know what men of the past thought, because we appreciate that all increase of knowledge comes by an evolutionary process advancing stage by stage, but our emphasis will always be on the facts accurately observed, and our ultimate appeal will always be to them.

Graduate and Undergraduate

One problem that was not solved in Harper's day and has not been solved since is that of the relationship between less advanced and more advanced students, whether these are thought of as students in "junior college" and "senior college," or as "undergraduates" and "graduates." Reference has already been made to the attempt to deal with this through organization of two separate divisions, and Dr. Strong's vigorous denunciation of any plan that involved carrying on both undergraduate and graduate work in the same institution.[47] It was President Harper's hope, as formulated in *Official Bulletin No. 2*, that by dividing the four-year period into an "Academic College" (freshman and sophomore years) and the "University College" (junior and senior years), it would be possible "to distinguish sharply between the earlier and later parts of the college course; to prevent attendance on the same courses of men of different maturity; to secure to every student, even in a large institution, all the advantages of the smaller colleges; to afford an opportunity to men from other institutions to do work in their junior and senior years more distinctly of university character."

Thirty years after the founding of the University, President Burton wrote:

The University of Chicago was thought of by its founders as a college. Before it opened its doors, however, their ideal had, under the influence

[47] Cf. supra, pp. 94, 116.

of President Harper's dominant personality, been displaced by that of a university, in which graduate work should hold the place of eminence, but in which undergraduates should also have place and consideration. Thus for thirty years on the same quadrangles, and in the same buildings, to a certain extent in the same classes and under the same professors, graduates and undergraduates have done their work side by side. That there are advantages in this plan need not be denied. But that it has serious disadvantages is beyond dispute. The ideals and purposes of a graduate school are in important respects different from those which properly characterize college work, and the total atmosphere of the two divisions of the University ought to be different. So marked has our sense of this fact become that some have even proposed either that we should do away with our Colleges or concentrate attention upon our graduate work to an extent that would inevitably spell deterioration for the Colleges.[48]

The fact is, of course, that the problem thus posed has proved to be much more complicated than it appeared to be to President Harper and others at Chicago. For one thing, it has had to be recognized as much more than an organizational matter. In nearly all the discussions of the time a quantitative concept of education was tacitly accepted, with a gradation based on number of years of subject matter covered.[49] Such a concept would be more and more questioned today, or at least modified considerably with special reference to mental and emotional maturity as the determining factor in admission to "advanced work" rather than years spent and courses "passed." The experience at Swarthmore, Reed, and many other four-year colleges, as well as at the University of Chicago and elsewhere, would be cited as evidence of the ability of "undergraduates" under certain conditions to meet the most exacting intellectual standards and achieve the independence assumed to be characteristic of graduate work.

PRESIDENT HARPER'S CONTRIBUTION

If Chicago in the early days came no nearer solving this pressing question of relationship between advanced and elementary (general) education, or the relation of "college" work to "graduate" work, at least President Harper

[48] University of Chicago, *President's Report*, 1922–1923, pp. xv–xvi.

[49] See, for example, the *President's Report*, University of Chicago, for 1910–1911, pp. 13–14. Dean George A. Works points out that, "as far as terminology is concerned," the matter has been settled in the University of Chicago by calling the two groups "college" and "divisional" students. He adds: "By and large the Division students are handled essentially as if they were graduate students, and we have a number of cases each year of students who go on to advanced degrees without taking the Bachelor's degree at all." (Letter of June 7, 1939.)

was able to instill ideals of high quality in every department of the University. Professor Joseph Henry Beale, Jr., who served at both Chicago and Harvard, and concluded from his experiences that the Chicago plan of division into two parts would ultimately be the base on which universities of the future would organize themselves, nevertheless placed much greater stress on President Harper's own devotion and enthusiasm than on any plan of organization. "No man ever came into contact with Dr. Harper to work along with him," says Professor Beale, "without getting from him that touch of fire which enabled him to perform miracles of work." It was not, he says, by directing the details of their action, but "by stirring up their enthusiasm, by infusing into them some of his own enormous energy, that he was able to get the cooperation that was necessary to carry on his work, and it was thus that he achieved his success."[50]

This brings us once more, of course, to the question of the importance of one man's leadership and his possibly unique place in a given social enterprise. One of Harper's contemporaries, President Edmund James of the University of Illinois, asserted that "there never was a time in which he [Harper] did not dominate, in the good sense of that term, the situation—the whole situation, educational and financial—by his personality."[51] To a greater extent even than at Hopkins or Clark is it true for Chicago that the University would be almost unthinkable without William Rainey Harper.

Dr. John H. Finley once said that he found it necessary to think of three men, rather than one, in viewing what Harper had done:

The period of his active work after this phenomenally early preparation was only thirty years, including the first few years of apprenticeship, and the year at the end of his life, which was as a year of resurrection—a year of return to the earth. But the achievement of these three decades, begun at an immature age and crowned with the glory of the heroic struggle of the last year, was the achievement of three men, and of three extraordinary men. . . . Now it was teaching to which he gave himself with the strength of three men; another hour or another day it was to study, to the seeking of a scholar; and then the next hour or the next day it was the complex and tangled task of the executive to which this man of three men's brains set his hand. By this cooperation he accomplished what three men working independently, though of great ability each, could not have done. It seems as if nature had here exhibited in human life the wisdom

[50] *University Record*, March, 1906, pp. 18–19.
[51] Ibid., p. 26.

of combination and had given example of economy in the diversity of interest and effort.[52]

President Harper, however, hardly thought of himself as indispensable in the University development. As already noted, he was far from desirous of assuming the presidency. He had few illusions as to the office itself. In a paper prepared in 1904 but not published until many years after his death, he has left on record his own ideas of the functions of a university head.[53] What he wrote that year, close to the end of his career, depicts, not the director of a single advanced educational enterprise in its beginnings, but an overburdened executive charged with the management of a huge modern university whose complexities have become almost too great for any single individual to bear. "So numerous are the affairs of a great university," says Dr. Harper in this paper, "so heavy are they, in the responsibility which their conduct requires; so arduous, in the actual time required for their management; so heart-engrossing and mind-disturbing, that there is demanded for their adequate supervision a man possessing the strength of a giant and an intellectual capacity and moral courage of the most determined character":

> One, indeed, possessed of strength, feels himself weak when he is brought face to face with all that is demanded; and one becomes sick at heart when he contemplates how much additional strength is needed to enable him to fulfill his duties as his conscience tells him they should be fulfilled.

Periods of "utter dissatisfaction with one's own work" are the lot of the administrator as contrasted with that of the teacher:

> To what definite things can the president point and say—this is my work? Does he not find his highest function in helping others to do the things which he himself would like to do? Yet he must stand aside and see others take up this very work which in his heart he would desire to handle. The head of an institution is not himself permitted to finish a piece of work.

Professor Shorey points out that the demands upon President Harper's vitality were terrific, "for, though he never stinted his service to the University, he could not bring himself to renounce his other activities":

> With all these other interests on his mind he not only administered the

---

[52] Ibid., p. 51. Also, in part, in Thomas W. Goodspeed, *William Rainey Harper*, pp. 1–2.

[53] "William Rainey Harper. The College President" in *The Educational Record*, 19:178–186, April, 1938.

University, foresaw its successive developments, but he labored under the constant strain of the sense that everything thus far acccomplished was precarious and could be secured only by pressing forward. Everything depended, he felt, on his own unrelaxing vigilance, and on his continuing power to interest, persuade, lead, guide, and it might be cajole.[54]

Those who knew Dr. Harper say that his imagination was a conspicuous feature—it was "vivid, retentive, creative." On the other hand, Dr. Vincent asserts, "this almost exuberant imagination was disciplined and controlled by a keen, analytical intelligence and a capacity for generalization."

His scholarship was careful and conscientious. His mind worked methodically as well as brilliantly. . . . His powers of assimilation were extraordinary. . . . He realized his ideal of a university president, a scholar among scholars, interested in their studies as well as his own.[55]

His "disciplined imagination," Vincent further says, generated enthusiasm everywhere. "People were fond of calling him dynamic, and with reason." The mental image of a new idea, a plan to be realized, stirred in him an intense emotional urge. Doubtless Goodspeed had this in mind when he compared President Gilman's planning at Hopkins with the Harper plan at Chicago—anything that was not born alive and whole did not seem possible to Harper.

That Dr. Harper was essentially a teacher is the judgment of most of those who knew him. "The scholar, the administrator, and the leader was preeminently a teacher," says Albion W. Small. "Teaching was his chosen profession, and this would have been his preference, as he frequently said, if he had been obliged to choose between the presidency and a professorship in the University of Chicago."[56] Administrative duties were thrust upon him and he could not escape. "Teaching was to him a delight," says Dr. Judson, "he threw himself into it with eager enthusiasm." But he was also an investigator. With him the only question was, is it true? "His cardinal canons of research [in Hebrew] were identical with those of men of science." Not only that, but truth possessed him. "It was not laid away ticketed on the shelf of the museum. It was the very life of his life—it was himself. Hence came the tremendous force of his advocacy of any cause. Scientific truth which seemed to have no bearing on bettering human conditions did not appeal to him."[57]

[54] *Dictionary of American Biography*, vol. VIII, p. 289.

[55] George E. Vincent, "William Rainey Harper," *William Rainey Harper Memorial Conference.* Chicago, University of Chicago Press, 1938, p. 20.

[56] Albion W. Small, "As University Professor," *Biblical World*, March, 1906, p. 192.

[57] *University Record*, March, 1906, p. 10.

Toward the close of his eulogy of Dr. Harper, uttered many years after his death, Dr. George E. Vincent emphasized Harper's courage:

His courage was steadfast and rose at the end to heroism. He went forward amid difficulties which would have disheartened most men; he was steady and confident in threatening crises; he held himself to almost overwhelming tasks. He inspired others with his unfaltering belief which denied the possibility of defeat.

These outstanding traits and other more elusive qualities combined to form and animate a notable and potent personality who did momentous things for scholarship and education. Oblivion quickly overtakes even the conspicuous figures of any period. Only to a rare few is an enduring place in history assured. William Rainey Harper was one of these. No true record of American education can omit his name.[58]

In view of all the circumstances, the connection between Johns Hopkins University and Clark University, and Clark itself with Chicago, President G. Stanley Hall's statement in one of the Harper memorial volumes seems especially significant, not only as an estimate of Dr. Harper but also as a summary of some of the achievements at the University of Chicago in the early days:

I long ago came to admire President Harper's genius, and yield to no man in appreciation of his masterly work and of the great institution he has established. All the way from university extension and summer schools for teachers to the very highest graduate study and research, he has done pioneer and epoch-making work, and made all universities his debtors for original plans, and has found or made a way to the practical realization of many a scheme which older and more conservative institutions piously wished to realize, but could hardly have achieved in a generation. The influence of all he did on the seaboard institutions will be a brilliant chapter in the future history of higher education.[59]

To this should be added President Faunce's words from the *University Record*:

Wealth alone is powerless to establish a seat of learning. It can no more create a university than it can create a human being. We may put millions into a treasury and the heart of youth still be unstirred, the force of scholarship still be silent, and the fountains of inspiration still be sealed. But when the man comes who can take our gold and by his insight, foresight,

---

[58] In *Proceedings of the William Rainey Harper Memorial Conference*, 1937, pp. 21–22.
[59] *Biblical World*, March, 1906, pp. 233–234.

and energy transmute it into the fellowship of scholars, into the eager pursuit of truth whether it lead to joy or pain, into undying allegiance to the ideal and the eternal, then satisfying wealth follows the man as the tides unswervingly follow the moon.[60]

---

[60] *University Record*, March, 1906, pp. 4–5.

SUMMARY AND CONCLUSIONS

IT seems clear that the unusual success of the pioneering efforts of the three universities whose beginnings are reviewed in this study came about largely because those in charge recognized the urgency of certain needs in higher education that were not being met by the conventional college education of the day; because, moreover, in striving to meet these needs those in authority had the wisdom to place the human element in the educational process, the students and faculty, ahead of buildings, enrollments, administration, and organization; and because the men who headed the universities were themselves vigorous personalities who insisted upon the highest possible quality of intellect and character in the institutions they directed.

Undoubtedly other factors entered into the achievement of Johns Hopkins, Clark, and the University of Chicago in the early days, but these three—the determination to meet real needs rather than follow a pattern, emphasis on persons rather than things, and insistence upon quality—were outstanding. To what extent they apply to present conditions in higher education, especially at the graduate level, can only be determined by those who have to deal in a practical way with individual institutions. Of their significance for these three universities in the beginning years there can hardly be any question.

MEETING THE NEEDS OF SOCIETY

All three of the universities began with the very definite conviction that American colleges and universities were not meeting the needs of society, and that fundamental changes were necessary. "A new institution on a new plan," was President Gilman's announced intention at Baltimore. From the start the Johns Hopkins University was committed to "the most liberal promotion of all useful knowledge," to provision for departments of learning "elsewhere neglected in the country"; to enlargement of the resources of American scholarship and encouragement of research; and particularly to "studies which bear upon life,"—that is, not only the biological sciences just then coming into prominence, but the "modern humanities" as well, with their concern for man in relation to society. Indeed, President Gilman himself conceived of higher education as in large part an effort to achieve, through intellectual and moral growth, a "better state of society than now exists." He was impressed with the risk universities run of falling into ruts, and was convinced that almost any epoch in higher education requires a fresh start.

At Clark the determination to face a new educational task was even more definite. President G. Stanley Hall had left Baltimore to go to Worcester only on the assurance that he was not to head a conventional New England college but rather to establish a new kind of university that would be "a leader and a light." Indeed, he intended that Clark should symbolize a more serious break with the traditional higher institution in America than Johns Hopkins had been; Clark was to be a specialized advanced institution even more exclusively graduate and research in type than Hopkins. It was to select only the best students, train leaders, and advance science by new discoveries. Whatever the real aspirations of Mr. Jonas Clark, the founder, may have been, President Hall had his mind set on a new movement in American higher education and the part Clark was to play in it. He spoke feelingly of the tendency of endowed institutions to cease to be productive, to become dry, formal, sterile. We need, he said, in this country "new men, new measures, and occasionally new universities." Even when the anticipated resources failed to materialize and Clark University was compelled to reduce its program to only a fraction of the original, so firmly did Hall and his associates keep this principle in mind that competent educational observers of the day were able to say that Clark had made possible new lines of scientific research, widened the confines of human knowledge, and successfully challenged the aims and purposes of contemporary education.

The attempt to meet significant needs of the times in higher education was conspicuously evident at the University of Chicago. President Harper viewed his enterprise as a "unique departure" in American education, designed to meet, still more directly than the Johns Hopkins University had done, certain needs of the day. It is impossible to read the correspondence and reports that preceded the founding of the new University of Chicago without realizing that those who were working for the University, even when they talked about it as a Baptist undertaking, were in reality seeking to meet needs in advanced education that were not being met adequately anywhere. In all President Harper's detailed plans for changes in organization— the four-quarter plan, the requirement of majors and minors, the lessened instructional schedule—the underlying purpose was to free the University from the handicaps of the traditional college and thereby stimulate scholarship and research. Dr. Harper was at times a most severe critic of the American college system; he argued that it had "actually destroyed the intellectual growth of thousands of strong and able men." He sought to build a university that would provide a "center of thought on every problem connected with human life and work," that would be accepted by the people as an

agency designed to help them solve the problems of civilization—a place where
conscious effort should be made to guide the people in deciding fundamental
questions on the basis of discovered truth. He insisted that the most distinctive characteristic of nineteenth century university development was
adaptation of university methods and training to the practical problems of
the age, and the consequent obligation resting upon the universities to be
systematically represented in the many new fields of knowledge opened up
by modern civilization.

Especially with respect to what all three universities called "research"
there seems to have been a much more specific sense of responsibility for
human welfare and the needs of society than came to be associated with
university research activities at a later period. Insistence at all three universities upon research as essential for the everyday work of teaching and as
the test for professional advancement can be understood only in the light
of a creative kind of research as opposed to the routines involved in a conventional doctoral dissertation.

Men Before Buildings

That universities are made possible by men rather than buildings was a
principle insisted upon in all three of these pioneering institutions in their
early days. At Johns Hopkins the donor's sole condition—that the capital
gift must not be used for construction of plant—helped to place the emphasis
immediately upon the human beings in the educational enterprise. Contemporary accounts agree that teachers and students were put ahead of everything else at Baltimore. The faculty were selected on the basis of their devotion to a particular line of study and assurance of eminence in it, the power
to pursue independent investigation and inspire young students with enthusiasm for study and research, and certain personal characteristics deemed
necessary for a wholesome relationship between teachers and students. The
students were also selected with care, usually through acquaintance with
staff members of colleges and universities elsewhere. Survivors of the early
Hopkins days say that President Gilman would have been glad to travel
across the continent to make sure of a man of value for one of his fellowships.
In President Nicholas Murray Butler's words, Gilman knew that for a university "you had to have men," and he went out and got the men. How
effective the Johns Hopkins selection of students must have been is partly
indicated by the fact that the Baltimore institution soon came to be the
place from which faculty were recruited for Harvard, Yale, and other Ameri-

can universities. Of sixty-nine persons who received the doctor's degree from Hopkins in the first ten years, fifty-six secured positions on the staffs of thirty-two universities and colleges.

At Clark emphasis upon selection of faculty and students was equally marked. Even President G. Stanley Hall's severest critics testified to his skill in selecting "an extraordinarily gifted group of men,"—so gifted that President William Rainey Harper found in them the nucleus for one of his strongest faculty groups at the University of Chicago. Few would question the accuracy of Hall's statement that he had managed to bring together at Clark for certain departments of study and research a teaching force "then nowhere equalled in the country." Students, likewise, were drawn to Clark University on the theory that here was a place for those who were really talented and could take part in the special graduate opportunities provided.

At the University of Chicago an inordinate amount of President Harper's time and energy went into the task of selecting the high type of faculty those behind the new university considered indispensable. They acted on the principle that "it is men and nothing but men that make education."

Conditions of Teaching and Learning

This concern for careful selection of faculty and students was accompanied in all three institutions by an insistence upon conditions of teaching and learning that encouraged independent investigation, intimate and informal teacher-student relationship, and a minimum of administrative machinery. At the end of fifteen years President Gilman was convinced that what had brought students to Johns Hopkins was "not halls nor books, nor instruments, important as these are," but expectations that the methods of instruction would be stimulating, inspiring, and strengthening; that a strong personal interest would be shown in every student; that the companionship of scholars brought together from every part of the land, with diverse tastes, attainments, and tendencies would make an intellectual microcosm in which it would be profitable to dwell. Graduate students at Hopkins found awaiting them easy access to distinguished teachers and companionship with mature minds. Every possible method of teaching and learning seems to have been used, with individual conference and seminar especially prominent.

At Clark University there was the same emphasis upon informal conditions of teaching and learning; Hall and his associates found the highest possible intellectual aims wholly compatible with friendliness and sympathetic concern for the individual. Reliable observers insist that at Clark every student was made to feel that he stood for something, that teachers were even greater as friends than as pedagogues, and that those in charge had "faith in men and friendship for men." It is to the close personal relations between professors and students that many commentators attribute the long-continued Clark success. President Hall was determined that students should be personally aided, guided to the best literature, and advanced by every method that pedagogic skill and sympathy could devise. The very attitude of research, Dr. Hall believed, gave teaching a new power and zest; students had a right, he felt, to the "heat and light" that accompany discovery on the part of a teacher who is also a creative research worker. He thought the student needed to have the thrill of discovery that goes with the search for independent knowledge. Stated lectures were a minor part of the Clark program; instead, reliance was placed upon "elbow-teaching" in the laboratory, individual guidance, clubs, conferences, and seminaries—especially the seminary conducted for many years by G. Stanley Hall himself, of the virtues of which survivors from the old Worcester days seldom speak without exaggeration.

Freedom of teaching and learning was inherent in these pioneer beginnings. It is doubtful if any stronger words for university freedom have ever been uttered than those of President William Rainey Harper of the University of Chicago. A faculty composed of individuals of widely differing views were brought together at Chicago and were expected to be independent in their research and free in their teaching. The principle of "complete freedom of speech on all subjects" was insisted upon from the first, and President Harper stated as explicitly as he could that no donor had the right to interfere with the teaching in the university. Even though this freedom of speech might be abused, he said, there was no justification for curtailing it: "the abuse of it is not so great an evil as the restriction of such liberty."

At Johns Hopkins the same attitude prevailed. What was conceived of from the beginning was a faculty free to teach and carry on research, and a student body correspondingly unrestricted. It was assumed that in the kind of university Hopkins set out to be the faculty would necessarily comprise men for whom liberty of teaching and research was imperative, and the effort constantly was to create, in President Remsen's words, "an atmosphere good to live in, an atmosphere salutary and stimulating." At least one observer felt that because of this condition, members of the faculty at Hopkins were even more creative and productive than their previous record would have indicated they might be.

At Clark University, despite the difficulties that developed early in the relationships of the faculty and the president, there was never any question as to the almost ideal conditions of freedom of teaching and learning that prevailed. Hall in later years told with pardonable pride of the way young men who studied at Clark, even in the days of most limited resources, "grew intellectually as if by leaps and bounds." One of the original group at Clark reflected accurately the Clark spirit when he said that the answer to the question as to the success of Hopkins, Clark, and Chicago was not only men of ability, professors and students with sufficient resources to carry on their work, but time for research and "freedom to work in their own way."

Individual Personalities

One inevitable question in all this has to do with the individuals who headed the three universities in their pioneering days. To what extent was the success of each of these institutions due to the leadership exerted by Gilman at the Johns Hopkins, Hall at Clark, and Harper at the University of Chicago?

It goes almost without saying that each of these universities could hardly have developed in the particular form it did if it had had some other individual as president. This does not necessarily mean that the three universities would not have succeeded without these three men, but they would have been different. In any case, the principle of persons as more significant than physical externals is again evident here. It was no accident that men of the quality of Gilman, Hall, and Harper headed these institutions; they were selected for the tasks because in every case those behind the new enterprise could not conceive of its succeeding without leadership of a high order. The trustees of the Johns Hopkins University, for example, gave largely of their time to search for the type of man they needed, and when they found him they encouraged and helped him in every way to exert his educational leadership. Experts in university administration have said that Daniel Coit Gilman was probably the best equipped man to head a pioneering university that could have been found; that the success of the Johns Hopkins University was in considerable measure due to the happy circumstance that a great educational gift fell into the hands of a man who by training and experience was in close touch with the education and scholarship of his day.

At Clark, similarly, although G. Stanley Hall had not had the administrative experience and broad acquaintance with university affairs that Gilman had had, the first president was a distinguished scientist of his time, selected for the Clark post as a direct result of his connection with Johns Hopkins. The impress of his personality on Clark University was unmistakable. He made the University according to his own plans. After the first three years, when it became evident that the funds anticipated for a comprehensive graduate university would not be forthcoming at Worcester, Hall made his own special contribution as the leader of a small group of teachers and research workers, demonstrating dramatically what can be done with minimum resources when there is determination to maintain intellectual standards of a high order. Doubtless Clark University would have been a different place if Hall had not continued to head it; but, on the other hand, there were other personalities in the Worcester venture, and perhaps the most that can be said is that at least some of the qualities Dr. Hall had would have been essential to any outstanding achievement.

At the University of Chicago William Rainey Harper was definitely "drafted" for the presidency. All the preliminary planning pointed so clearly to Harper's leadership that it is especially difficult to think of anyone other than Harper heading the new enterprise. One of his biographers has put on record the conviction that for at least a quarter of a century after his death the University of Chicago was the embodiment of Harper's spirit. Nevertheless, Dr. Harper would probably have repudiated any suggestion that he was indispensable to the University, insisting, rather, that the program he was working for was one that included necessary steps for any institution seeking to meet the needs of the day in higher education.

In all three of the universities reviewed in this study there were various elements in the program that had special bearing on the success of the university in its pioneering days—at Hopkins, for example, the use of outside lecturers and the establishment of the scholarly journals; at Clark President Hall's seminary; at Chicago the development of the University of Chicago Press. The small numbers of the early days were a distinct advantage. But the factors that counted most heavily seem to have been the three that have been stressed in this concluding section—the effort to make university education more adequately meet the needs of the times; the precedence given to the human beings in the educational enterprise—teachers and students—rather than buildings, equipment, and administrative machinery, together with conditions of teaching and learning that go with this emphasis upon persons; and the placing of educational leadership in the hands of highly qualified men carefully selected for their knowledge of education and determined to have the highest possible quality in the educational process.

BIBLIOGRAPHY

A selected list of books and articles having to do with the early days of the Johns Hopkins University, Clark University, and the University of Chicago.

THE JOHNS HOPKINS UNIVERSITY

Bond, Allen Kerr. When the Hopkins came to Baltimore. Baltimore, Maryland, Pegasus press, 1927. 84 p.

A first-hand account by a Baltimore physician who as a youth attended the collegiate department of the Hopkins in 1876 (the second undergraduate examined for admission), and describes the faculty, student body, and episodes of the early days.

Butler, Nicholas Murray. President Gilman's administration at the Johns Hopkins university. American monthly review of reviews, 23:49–53, January 1901.

Analyzes the elements in the Johns Hopkins success—President Gilman himself as the man who organized and guided; real understanding of what a "university" was and determination to create one; emphasis upon men, rather than buildings; the annual fellowships open to graduates of any college; the opportunity for research and publication. Johns Hopkins University, Dr. Butler concludes "has held up new ideals, suggested new methods, enforced new and high standards of excellence and achievement."

Dorfman, Joseph. Thorstein Veblen and his America. New York, The Viking press, 1934.

Describes Veblen's not altogether favorable impressions of the Johns Hopkins of his student days, which he considered "not what he had been led to expect by the circulars of information." Recognizes valuable elements but stresses certain weaknesses.

Flexner, Abraham. Address. *In* Symposium on the outlook for higher education in the United States. Proceedings of the American philosophical society, 69:257–269, no. 5, 1930. Lancaster, Pennsylvania, Lancaster press inc., 1930.

Characterizes the Johns Hopkins in the early days as "a genuine university in its efforts and in its ideals: the only university, in fact the only institution, expressly and mainly devoted to the advancement of learning which at that time existed in this country."

Flexner, Abraham. The prepared mind. School and society, 45:865–872, June 26, 1937.

Discusses the need for simplification of American university education and pays tribute to Johns Hopkins University as an example of practical educational procedure in the direction of "the prepared mind."

Flexner, Abraham. Universities, American, English, German. New York, Oxford university press, 1930. 381 p.

Contains numerous references to the Johns Hopkins University. Discussing the development of graduate schools, Dr. Flexner says: "The most distinctive American graduate school was started in Baltimore in 1876, largely under the influence of the German universities. It began with a faculty of philosophy and shortly afterwards with a single professional faculty, that of medicine, both under the leadership of a great and scholarly president. At its beginning and for twenty years thereafter the

Johns Hopkins University was the nearest thing to a university and practically nothing else that America has yet possessed."

Franklin, Fabian. The life of Daniel Coit Gilman. New York, Dodd, Mead, and co., 1910. 446 p.

Two of the main chapters in this biography (p. 182–219), are devoted to an account of President Gilman's career at the Johns Hopkins, and the earlier chapters—describing Gilman's European travel, his various activities at Yale University, including his work at the School of Science and the library, and his three years as president of the University of California—are important for understanding his development of the work at the Hopkins.

Many original memoranda are made available in this book, for example, the notes of the first meeting (in 1874) between Mr. Gilman and the Johns Hopkins trustees in which Mr. Gilman told the trustees, in substance, that "he would make it [the new university] the means of promoting scholarship of the first order, and this by only offering the kind of instruction to advanced students which other universities offer in their postgraduate courses, and leaving the kind of work now done by undergraduates to be done elsewhere."

An account is given of the method of selecting the first faculty; of the establishment of journals at Hopkins devoted to research; of the notable program of lectures by visiting scholars; of the establishment of the Hospital and Medical School; of the connection between the University and social service.

French, John C. Johns Hopkins, founder. The Johns Hopkins alumni magazine, 25:227–234, March 1937.

The man whose philanthropy created the Johns Hopkins opportunity is strangely forgotten, says Dr. French in this summary of the main facts of the life and work of Johns Hopkins, merchant of Baltimore.

Gilman, Daniel Coit. The launching of a university. New York, Dodd, Mead, and co., 1906. 386 p.

Eight of the papers in this collection deal directly with Johns Hopkins University: I. Reminiscences of thirty years in Baltimore, 1875–1905; II. Johns Hopkins and the trustees of his choice; III. Fundamental principles; IV. The original faculty; V. Some noteworthy teachers no longer living; VI. Publication; VII. The Johns Hopkins medical school; VIII. Resignation, a farewell address, February 22, 1902. President Gilman says: "I have the advantage of knowing more than anyone else of an unwritten chapter of history; the disadvantage of not being able or disposed to tell the half that I remember."

Gilman, Daniel Coit. Scientific schools in Europe. Barnard's journal of education, March 1856.

This is a detailed description of scientific schools in Saxony, Belgium, Prussia, Austria, and France, "considered in reference to their prevalence, utility, scope and desirability in America," and is of interest as indicating Gilman's early concern (he was 25 when he wrote it) for higher scientific education in the United States.

Gilman, Daniel Coit. University problems in the United States. New York, The century co., 1898. 319 p.

Two addresses in this volume deal directly with the early days of Johns Hopkins: The first (p. 1–44) is the inaugural address of Gilman as president of the Johns Hopkins University in 1876. The second is a discourse of 1885, designed to furnish a "new exposition" of the principles and aims of the university.

Gilman, Daniel Coit. *In* Dictionary of American biography, New York, Charles Scribner's sons, 1931, vol. VII, p. 299–303.

Gives considerable information in small space on the early days of the Johns Hopkins University. Describes particularly the selection of faculty.

Gilman, Daniel Coit, first president of Johns Hopkins university, 1876–1901. Baltimore, The Johns Hopkins university press, 1908. (The Johns Hopkins university circular, no. 5, 1908, no. 10; whole number 211; December 1908.)

This issue of the Johns Hopkins university circular contains commemoratory addresses by Dr. Ira Remsen, Ambassador James Bryce, Dr. William H. Welch, Professor Basil L. Gildersleeve, and others; together with letters from university heads, and an article from "The Nation" by Dr. Fabian Franklin (later incorporated in the biography of Gilman by Franklin).

Hall, G. Stanley. Johns Hopkins university. *In his* Life and confessions of a psychologist. New York, D. Appleton and co., 1927. p. 225–257.

Dr. Hall reviews in an interesting personal way his experiences at Baltimore, where, he says, "the University at that time was adding another story to our educational system." He describes the work of Charles Peirce; gives an account of his own activities as "professor of psychology and pedagogy" (the latter part of the title bestowed against his wishes); mentions some of the students he had— John Dewey, J. McKeen Cattell, H. H. Donaldson, W. H. Burnham, Joseph Jastrow, and others; relates stories of Professor Rowland, H. Newell Martin, Gildersleeve, "the famous Hellenist"; and explains the difficult social situation involved in locating a university in Baltimore in the 70's. He discusses interestingly, also, the "religious barrier to complete sympathy."

Huxley, Thomas Henry. An address on the occasion of the opening of the Johns Hopkins university. *In his* American addresses, New York, D. Appleton and co., 1877. p. 100–127.

Having paid tribute to the creation of the Johns Hopkins University as something unique in educational history, Huxley sets out to see how far the principles underlying the enterprise "are in accordance with those which have been established in my own mind by much and long continued thought upon educational questions." He makes the point that "university education should not be something distinct from elementary education, but should be the natural outgrowth and development of the latter."

Ingle, Edward. The first ten years at Johns Hopkins. The Johns Hopkins alumni magazine, 4:7–26, November 1915.

Gives many details of the early years: Numbers of students; what students have done since graduation; the scientific achievements of workers at the university; the building plans; student life; outside visitors and lecturers; the scholarly publications sponsored by the university.

John, Walton C. Graduate study in universities and colleges in the United States. Washington, Government printing office, 1935. 234 p. (Office of education bulletin, 1934, no. 20.)

Discusses the beginnings of graduate study in American higher institutions, and includes some mention of the early days of Johns Hopkins. The bulletin says: "The establishment of Johns Hopkins University in 1876 under the leadership of Gilman gave extraordinary impetus to the true concept of a university and became a rapidly working leaven in a number of state as well as privately controlled universities."

Johns Hopkins half-century directory, 1876–1926. Baltimore, The Johns Hopkins
university press, 1926. 542 p.

By means of this comprehensive list of "trustees, faculty, holders of honorary degrees, and students,
graduates and non-graduates" it is possible to get some measure of the quality of those connected
with the University in its early days.

Johns Hopkins university. Addresses at the inauguration of Daniel C. Gilman as
president of the Johns Hopkins university. Baltimore, John Murphy and co.,
1876. 64 p.

Includes a description of the public exercises connected with the inauguration on February 22, 1876;
the "congratulatory address" by President Charles W. Eliot, of Harvard University; and President
Gilman's inaugural address.

Johns Hopkins university. Annual report of the president. Baltimore, 1876 to
date.

President Gilman's annual reports are full of directly valuable information and statements of policy,
much of which has been reproduced in *Launching of a University* and in Fabian Franklin's biography
of Gilman. This material also forms the basis for most of the short articles on the early days of the
Johns Hopkins that appear in Bernard C. Steiner's *History of University Education in Maryland*
and elsewhere.

  Particularly illuminating for university policies are the first, second, third, tenth, and twentieth
reports. The third annual report contains a discussion of the underlying principles in the light of
the experience of the first two years. In the twentieth annual report (1896–97) one finds a careful
review of the whole Johns Hopkins experiment up to that time.

Johns Hopkins university. Celebration of the twenty-fifth anniversary of the founding of the university and inauguration of Ira Remsen as president of the university. Baltimore, Johns Hopkins university press, 1902. 182 p.

Includes statements by university presidents comparing the work of the first Johns Hopkins period
with what was likely to come after. President Harper, of Chicago, expected to see the higher work
of universities more clearly separated from the lower work of the college; President Remsen thought
that advancing the age of graduation from college was interfering with scholarship in the highest
sense; and President Butler, of Columbia University, warned against overemphasis on degrees in
the attempt to solve the university-college problem.

Lowell, A. Lawrence. Universities, graduate schools, and colleges. *In his* At war
with academic traditions in America. Cambridge, Harvard university press,
1933. p. 206–220.

Conceding that "Daniel Coit Gilman did a great work, making in the highest ranges of education
the largest single advance in the annals of our country," President Lowell nevertheless calls attention to what he considers the unfortunate results that came from concern for degrees at Johns Hopkins, the effect of graduate schools in blocking the advance of the college, and other developments
since the days of the Johns Hopkins University that have placed, as he conceives it, undue emphasis
on the graduate school as compared with the college.

Malone, Kemp. Some observations on Gilman's Hopkins. Johns Hopkins alumni
magazine, 19:303–320, June 1931.

A reply to certain of the comments of Dr. Abraham Flexner in his book *Universities—English,*

American, German, and to other observers who, in Professor Malone's opinion, tend to look upon the administration of President Gilman as a kind of Golden Age, "an age which the unworthy present might revere but might not hope to surpass or even equal."

Thomas, James Carey. Brief review of the ten years' work of the Johns Hopkins university. Baltimore, John Murphy and co., 1886. 15 p.

This address by one of the early trustees gives a clear statement of the purposes behind the university as seen by the members of the board and the extent to which these had been realized by the end of the first decade. Dr. Thomas answers the question of the Johns Hopkins achievement in terms of (1) quality of teachers; (2) university courses and graduate students; (3) laboratory and other materials; (4) research and publication; (5) value of the training; (6) contributions of the university to the community.

CLARK UNIVERSITY

American journal of psychology, July–October, 1903 (Vol. 14, p. 1–430).

A commemorative number containing twenty-five articles by American and European psychologists "dedicated conjointly by colleagues and former pupils" of G. Stanley Hall.

Atwood, Wallace W. The first fifty years. Worcester, Mass., Clark university, 1937. 120 p.

A convenient short account of Clark University. Includes a foreword dealing with the original purpose and present status of the University; an historical sketch by Dr. George H. Blakeslee; accounts of the Graduate School of Geography, the College, the library, and the summer school, together with an explanation of Clark University funds, particularly the four endowments resulting from the gifts of Mr. and Mrs. Jonas G. Clark.

Clark university. Annual reports of the president to the board of trustees, 1890 and thereafter (irregularly published). Worcester, Mass., published for the university.

Certain of the earlier and subsequent reports are rich in material explanatory of the origin and purposes of the university, and give detailed information about personnel, researches, and publications: First annual report, 1890, second annual report, 1891, third annual report, April 1893, reports for 1902 and for 1916.

Clark university, 1889–1899. Decennial celebration. Worcester, Mass., printed for the university, 1899. 566 p.

A memorial volume covering the first decade of Clark University, intended "to make the public acquainted with its aims and ideals, and with the character, scope, and amount of the work it has already done." Included in the volume are: A brief historical sketch; an account of the decennial celebration, with congratulatory speeches and letters; the decennial address by Dr. Hall; detailed descriptions of the contributions of the several departments of the University—mathematics, physics, biology, psychology (general psychology, psycho-pathology, anthropology, pedagogy, and philosophy), and the library; the scientific lectures delivered in connection with the decennial celebration; a list of the degrees conferred, 1881–1889; and the titles of published papers.

"The volume is intended," say William E. Story and Louis N. Wilson in the preface, "not only to commemorate the decennial anniversary of Clark University, but also to make the public acquainted with its aims and ideals and with the character, scope, and amount of the work it has already done."

Clark university. Early proceedings of the board of trustees. Press of the university, Worcester, Mass., 1901.

Includes papers dealing with the call and acceptance of President Hall; opinions of leading men of the day with regard to the work the new university should do; and addresses by Mr. Jonas Clark, Dr. Hall, and Senator George F. Hoar.

Fisher, Sara Carolyn. The psychological and educational work of Granville Stanley Hall. American journal of psychology, 36:1–52, January 1925.

Analyzes Hall's work in psychology and education, through both his writings and his activities at Clark University.

Granville Stanley Hall, February 1, 1844–April 24, 1924. In memoriam. Publications of the Clark university library, Worcester, Mass., vol. 7, no. 6, May 1925.

Contains a biographical sketch of Hall by Louis N. Wilson, accounts of Dr. Hall's work by Edmund C. Sanford and William H. Burnham, and tributes by many others, including Harry W. Chase, Frank J. O'Brien, and Lewis M. Terman.

Hale, Edward Everett. Clark university. In Tarry at home travels—1899. New England magazine, 39:243–246, October 1908.

Gives his impressions of an early meeting at Clark University and reflections on the changes in higher education that are suggested thereby.

Hall, G. Stanley. Life and confessions of a psychologist. New York, D. Appleton and co., 1927. 623 p.

Part of the impulse to write this autobiography, Dr. Hall says, was to "correct, so far as I could before I die, the long injustice done me by good men who did not and could not at the time know the relation of Mr. Clark to the institution he founded, which made the story of its first decade so unprecedentedly tragic."

Chapter VII, pages 258–334, is given over specifically to the experience at Clark University as seen by Dr. Hall himself. He describes the beginning of the university and his own connection with it, Mr. Clark's plans and ideas, the first European trip of exploration into higher educational methods, the changes that took place when it was evident resources were not going to be on the scale anticipated, the work in the "seminary," the migration of members of the faculty to Chicago, the scholarly journals associated with the Clark undertaking. The story is vividly told; details necessarily have to be checked with other accounts.

List of degrees granted at Clark university and Clark college, 1889–1920. Compiled by Louis N. Wilson. Publications of the Clark university library, Worcester, Mass., vol. 6, no. 3, December 1920.

Useful as indicating the caliber of the men who studied at Clark during the period covered.

Proceedings at the first annual banquet of the New England association of alumni of Clark university and at the banquet of the Washington, D. C., alumni association, 1907. Publications of the Clark university library, Worcester, Mass., vol. 2, no. 4, June 1907.

Includes tributes by alumni and others to the work at Clark University.

Pruette, Lorine. G. Stanley Hall, a biography of a mind. New York, D. Appleton and co., 1926. 267 p.

Analyzes the personality and work of Dr. Hall and includes considerable description of his activities at Clark University.

Sanford, Edmund C. A sketch of the history of Clark university. Publications of Clark university library, Worcester, Mass., vol. 7, no. 1, January 1923.

A brief account by one of the men who had much to do with both Clark University and Clark College with considerable attention to the earlier period.

Sheldon, H. D. Granville Stanley Hall. *In* Dictionary of American biography, New York, Charles Scribner's sons, 1932, vol. VIII, p. 127–130.

Gives excellent short account of the beginnings of Clark University, with discussion of Hall as an administrator and the part Hall played in the development of the University.

Starbuck, Edwin Dillon. G. Stanley Hall. Psychological review, 32:102–120, March 1925.

Summarizes the views of American psychologists, as recorded through questionnaires, on the contributions of Dr. Hall to psychology and education.

Stebbins, Calvin. Address at the founder's day exercises, February 1, 1905. Publications of the Clark university library, Worcester, Mass., vol. 1, no. 6, April 1905.

Gives some information regarding the life of Jonas Clark, founder of Clark University.

Thorndike, Edward Lee. Biographical memoir of Granville Stanley Hall. *In* National academy of sciences, vol. 12. Washington, D. C., The academy, 1929.

Includes analysis of Hall's work in psychology and some account of the early developments at Clark University.

Wilson, Louis N. G. Stanley Hall, a sketch. New York, G. E. Stechert, 1914. 144 p.

A fairly comprehensive outline of Hall's life and work up to 1914, with description of the beginnings and development at Clark University. Includes one of the first published accounts by Dr. Hall himself of the work of the seminary as he had conducted it in the first eight years.

Wilson, Louis N. Some recollections of our founder. Publications of the Clark university library, vol. 8, no. 2, February 1927.

Describes the life and work of Jonas Gilman Clark, founder of Clark University, giving numerous details of the early history of the University and Mr. Clark's connection with it. This is a particularly careful attempt to explain the differences in purposes that animated the two men most involved—Mr. Clark and President Hall.

Includes the text of the Act of incorporation of Clark University and the address of the Founder at the meeting of the Board of Trustees held May 4, 1887.

University of Chicago

Biblical world. March 1906. (Vol. 27, p. 161–252.)

This entire issue of a journal which Dr. Harper had founded was devoted to articles commemorating Harper's life and work. The articles include such titles as "The Granville Period," by E. Benjamin Andrews; "The Morgan Park Period," by Eri B. Hulbert; "The Yale Period," by Francis Knight Sanders; "The Chicago Period," by A. K. Parker; "In His Study," by John Merlin Powis Smith; "In the Field of Semitic Scholarship," by Emil G. Hirsch; "As University Professor," by Albion W. Small.

Flint, Nott William. The university of Chicago: a sketch. Chicago, The university of Chicago press, 1904. 14 p.

A short early account of the University which gives something of the history and contemporary organization of the institution.

Goodspeed, Thomas Wakefield. A history of the university of Chicago: the first quarter century. Chicago, University of Chicago press, 1916. 522 p.

Prepared by a man who, in President Harry Pratt Judson's words in the foreword, was "actively and zealously concerned from the outset—*pars magna fuit.*" Goodspeed's own connection with the movement resulting in the founding of the University of Chicago began in 1886 and his official relation to it began in June, 1889. Retired at age seventy, he was made corresponding secretary of the University and was asked by President Judson to write this history. He had also been a student in the first University of Chicago from 1859 to 1862 and trustee of the Theological Seminary, which became the Divinity School of the new University, from 1873 to 1889.

The book is particularly useful for the information it gives on the early development of the University, especially in its financial growth and the corresponding educational expansion.

Goodspeed, Thomas Wakefield. The story of the university of Chicago, 1890–1925. Chicago, University of Chicago press, 1925. 244 p.

This is a shorter volume, bringing down to 1925 the record of the University of Chicago which the author had given in considerably more detail in his larger history of 1916. Considerable space is given to the beginnings of the University, and especially Mr. Rockefeller's connection with it.

Goodspeed, Thomas Wakefield. William Rainey Harper. Chicago, University of Chicago press, 1928.

A detailed account, by the author of the two authorized histories of the University of Chicago, of the life and work of President William Rainey Harper, with numerous references to the origin and development of the University.

Harper, William Rainey. The college president. Educational record, 19:178–186, April 1938. (*Also in* The William Rainey Harper memorial conference, Chicago, University of Chicago press, 1938, p. 24–34.)

The manuscript of this article was found in the family files and read by Samuel N. Harper at the Muskingum conference of 1938. It had been prepared in 1904, but not published prior to the publication of the papers of the Muskingum conference. In the paper Dr. Harper discusses the difficulties and opportunities of a college and university president.

Harper, William Rainey. The trend in higher education. Chicago, University of Chicago press, 1905. 390 p.

This volume is the main source, outside of official university reports and bulletins, for President Harper's statements on what he was attempting at the University of Chicago and the relation of this to higher education generally in his time.

Hutchins, Robert Maynard. Inaugural address as president of the university of Chicago, November 19, 1929. Chicago, University of Chicago press, 1929.

Contains reference to President Harper's early purposes at the University of Chicago and the relation of these to subsequent developments in higher education at Chicago and elsewhere.

Montgomery, Robert N. (Ed.). The William Rainey Harper memorial conference. Chicago, University of Chicago press, 1938. 167 p.

This is an account of a conference held in connection with the centennial of Muskingum College, New Concord, Ohio, October 21-22, 1937. The contents include an address on President Harper by Dr. George E. Vincent, formerly president of the Rockefeller Foundation; a hitherto unpublished paper by President Harper on "The College President"; an "appreciation of William Rainey Harper," by John D. Rockefeller, Jr., and a short account by Dr. Vincent of the relationship of Mr. Rockefeller and President Harper.

Dr. Vincent's address dealt with three things, "first, William Rainey Harper's preparation for his life work; second, his ideal of a university which was approached by the University of Chicago; and, third, the qualities of mind and character which gave power and direction to his career."

Shorey, Paul. William Rainey Harper. *In* Dictionary of American biography, New York, Charles Scribner's sons, 1932, vol. VIII, p. 287-292.

Gives particular attention to Dr. Harper's connection with the University of Chicago and his influence on the institution.

Slosson, Edwin E. The university of Chicago. Independent, January 6, 1910, p. 21-41.

A popularly written account of what the author describes as "the youngest and greatest and most original" of three universities "raised from the seed" in modern times—the others being the Johns Hopkins and Leland Stanford.

Talbot, Marion. More than lore. Chicago, University of Chicago press, 1936. 223 p.

In these reminiscences Miss Talbot, dean of women at the University of Chicago from 1892 to her retirement in 1925, describes the University as she saw it in its beginnings; depicts the developing social life of the institution; and gives special attention to the faculty personalities of the early days.

The university of Chicago. Doctors of philosophy. Announcement, vol. 31, no. 19, May 15, 1931. Chicago, University of Chicago press.

Gives names and positions of those who received degree of doctor of philosophy, with title of dissertation in each case, from June 1893 to April 1931.

The university of Chicago. Official bulletin, nos. 1-6. Chicago, 1891-1893.

The first of these bulletins contains the original "Harper plan" as submitted by the committee on organization and faculty of the new University and adopted by the board of trustees on December 26th, 1890. It also includes two letters of John D. Rockefeller (May 15, 1889 and September 16, 1890) in which Mr. Rockefeller's two subscriptions of $600,000 and $1,000,000 were announced; names of the officers and board of trustees; the charter of the university; besides a description of the proposed activities and organization of the new institution.

Other bulletins dealt with specific aspects of the plan, including (bulletin number 4) the proposals for the graduate schools of the University.

156 BIBLIOGRAPHY

The university of Chicago. President's reports, July 1892–July 1902. Chicago, University of Chicago press, 1903.

This report material contains most of the significant statements President Harper made in connection with the planning and development of the University.

University record, March 1906.

This issue of the record is made up of memorial addresses following the death of President Harper. It includes statements from a number of the most distinguished educational leaders of the period, many of which go into the educational purposes and achievements of the University of Chicago in its early days.

INDEX

INDEX

Academic College, University of Chicago, 132.
Adams, Herbert B., 33, 44, 118.
Adler, Cyrus, 33.
Admission to graduate work
    Johns Hopkins, 33.
    University of Chicago, 113.
Adolescence, G. Stanley Hall's interest in, 82.
Agassiz, Louis, 7.
Aikins, H. Austin, 71.
Albee, Ernest, 71.
Alexander, S. D., 18.
Allen, William Francis, 41.
American Association of University Women, 119.
American Baptist Education Society, 93, 103, 104.
American Chemical Journal, 44.
American Institute of Sacred Literature, 106.
American Journal of Mathematics, 44, 45.
American Journal of Philology, 44.
American Journal of Psychology, 54, 90 note, 151.
American Journal of Semitic Languages and Literatures, 130.
American Journal of Sociology, 130.
Ames, Joseph S., 33, 36.
Anderson, G., 129.
Andrews, E. Benjamin, 110.
Angell, James Burrill, 10 note, 17, 130.
    On changes in higher education, 6.
    On Johns Hopkins presidency, 28 note.
Angell, J. R., 130.
Anthropology, at Clark University, 57.
Antioch College, G. Stanley Hall's experience in, 52.
Arnold, Matthew, 18.
Association of Collegiate Alumnae, 119.
Astronomy, research activities at Michigan, 10.
Astrophysical Journal, 130.
Atwood, Wallace W., 151.
Averill, Lawrence A., 81.

Bailey, Thomas P., Jr., 71.
Baltimore and Ohio Railroad, 16 note.
Baltimore City College, 19, 115.
Baptist Union Theological Seminary, 92, 108, 110.
Baptists, interest in education, 92, 95 ff., 97, 99, 116, 140.
    Attitude toward freedom of teaching, 127.
Barker, Lewellys Franklin, 121.
Barnard, Frederick A. P., 11, 68.

Barnes, Earl, 83.
Bassett, John Spencer, 33.
Bastian, Adolf, 53.
Beale, Joseph Henry, Jr., on William Rainey Harper, 134.
Beecher, Henry Ward, 51.
Bell, Alexander Graham, 42.
Benton, Thomas H., Jr., 32 note.
Bergson, Henri, 78.
Bergström, J. A., 72.
Berlin, University of, 93.
Biblical World, 130.
Bicknell, T. W., 3 note.
Billings, John Shaw, 41.
Biological science, as university study, 22, 25, 30, 114, 139.
Birkhoff, George D., 121.
Blakeslee, G. H., 73, 77, 83.
Blanchard, Phyllis M., 81.
Bloomfield, Maurice, 33.
Boas, Franz, 57, 71.
Boas, George, 45.
Bobbitt, John Franklin, 81.
Bolton, Frederick E., vii, 72, 81.
Bolton, Thaddeus L., 72, 81.
Bolza, Oskar, 56, 121.
Bond, Allen Kerr, on early days of the Johns Hopkins University, 15 note, 16, 147.
Book, William F., 81.
Botanical Gazette, 130.
Bowman, Isaiah, 34 note.
Brackett, Anna C., 18.
Bright, James W., 44.
Bristed, C. A., 18.
Brooks, W. K., 44.
Brown, E. N., 72.
Brown, George William, 17.
Brown University, graduate work, 4, 13.
Brünnow, Francis, 9, 10.
Bryan, William L., vii, 72, 81, 82.
    Concerning G. Stanley Hall, 83.
    Judgment on Clark University, 57.
    Opinion on G. Stanley Hall's seminar, 77.
Bryce, James, 42.
Bryn Mawr College, 17.
Bucke, W. Fowler, 81.
Buildings, university, 96.
    Clark University, 50, 58, 70, 71.
    Johns Hopkins University, 21.
    Subordinated to faculty and student needs, 139, 141.
    University of Chicago, 62.
Bulkley, Julia E., 119.

Human relationships in university activities, 142.
  At Clark University, 72.
Human values, in university education, 102.
  At Clark University, 88.
Hume, David, 78.
Hurlbut, Jesse L., 110.
Hutchins, Robert Maynard, 117, 155.
Huxley, Thomas, 22, 149.
  Address at opening of Johns Hopkins University, 24, 40.

INFORMALITY in higher education, at Johns Hopkins University, 34, 36.
Ingle, Edward, on conditions at Johns Hopkins University, 42, 44 note, 149.

JACKSON, C. L., 74 note.
James, Edmund, on William Rainey Harper, 134.
James, Henry, 5 note, 35 note, 39 note, 74 note.
James, William, 42, 47, 50.
Jameson, John Franklin, 121.
Jastrow, Joseph, 51.
Jessup, Walter A., vii.
John, Walton C., 149.
Johns Hopkins University, v, 3, 14, 15 ff., 94, 107, 111.
  Faculty, 34 ff.
  Influence on other higher institutions, 3, 39.
Johns Hopkins University Circular, 44.
Johnson, F., 129.
Johnson, Reverdy, Jr., 16, 18 note.
Journal of Geology, 130.
Journal of Physiology, 44.
Journal of Political Economy, 128, 130.
Journal of Religion, 130.
Journals, 90.
  Johns Hopkins University, 43 ff.
  University of Chicago, 130 ff.
Jowett's *Plato*, 78.
Judson, Harry Pratt, 121, 136.
  Comments on faculty at University of Chicago, 124.

KANT, Immanuel, *Critique of Pure Reason*, 78.
Keeler, James E., 42.
Kent, Sydney A., 117.
Keppel, Frederick P., 11 note.
Kimball, A. L., 36.
Kirkpatrick, E. A., 72.
Kirchmann, Julius H., 53.
Knapp, William I., 121.
Kolbe, Adolphe W. H., 53.
Kuhlmann, Fred, 81.
Krohn, William O., 72.

LADD, Christine, 118.
Ladd, George T., 106.
Langley, S. P., 42.
Lanier, Sidney, 42.
  Ode to the Johns Hopkins University, 15, 25.
Lanman, Charles R., 33.
  On selection of students at the Johns Hopkins University, 34 note.
Latané, John H., 33.
Latin language and literature, 114.
Laughlin, J. Laurence, 121, 128.
Law School, University of Chicago, 112.
Lawrence Scientific School, 13.
Lazarus, Moritz, 53.
Learned, Marion D., 33.
Lemon, James S., 72.
LeRossignol, James E., 72.
Leuba, James H., 72, 81.
Leuckart, Rudolf, 53.
Library facilities, Johns Hopkins University, 18.
Lillie, Frank R., vii, 63 note.
Lindley, Ernest H., vii, 81, 82.
Linn, James Weber, 111 note.
Locke, John, 78.
Loeb, Jacques, 121.
Lombard, Warren P., vii, 57, 63, 71.
Longfellow, Henry W., 7.
Lorimer, George C., 98.
Lowell, A. Lawrence, 150.
Lowell, James Russell, 8, 41, 42.
Ludwig, Carl F. W., 53, 72 note.

MAJORS and minors at the University of Chicago, 113.
Malone, Kemp, 21 note, 150.
Manly, John Matthews, 121.
Mann, Horace, 18.
March, Charles S., 11.
Marks, absence of at the Johns Hopkins University, 33.
Martin, H. Newell, 22, 44.
Maschke, Heinrich, 121.
Mateer, Florence, 81.
Mathematics as university study, 55, 114, 121.
McCosh, James, 13.
Mead, G. H., 130.
Medical School, University of Chicago, 112.
Mental hygiene as university study, 31.
Metaphysical Club, Johns Hopkins University, 45.
Methods of instruction at Clark University, 72 ff.
Meynert, Theodor, 53.
Michael, Arthur, 56.
Michelet, Karl L., 53.

AMERICAN EDUCATION:
ITS MEN, IDEAS, AND INSTITUTIONS
An Arno Press/New York Times Collection

Series I

Adams, Francis. **The Free School System of the United States.** 1875.

Alcott, William A. **Confessions of a School Master.** 1839.

American Unitarian Association. **From Servitude to Service.** 1905.

Bagley, William C. **Determinism in Education.** 1925.

Barnard, Henry, editor. **Memoirs of Teachers, Educators, and Promoters and Benefactors of Education, Literature, and Science.** 1861.

Bell, Sadie. **The Church, the State, and Education in Virginia.** 1930.

Belting, Paul Everett. **The Development of the Free Public High School in Illinois to 1860.** 1919.

Berkson, Isaac B. **Theories of Americanization: A Critical Study.** 1920.

Blauch, Lloyd E. **Federal Cooperation in Agricultural Extension Work, Vocational Education, and Vocational Rehabilitation.** 1935.

Bloomfield, Meyer. **Vocational Guidance of Youth.** 1911.

Brewer, Clifton Hartwell. **A History of Religious Education in the Episcopal Church to 1835.** 1924.

Brown, Elmer Ellsworth. **The Making of Our Middle Schools.** 1902.

Brumbaugh, M. G. **Life and Works of Christopher Dock.** 1908.

Burns, Reverend J. A. **The Catholic School System in the United States.** 1908.

Burns, Reverend J. A. **The Growth and Development of the Catholic School System in the United States.** 1912.

Burton, Warren. **The District School as It Was.** 1850.

Butler, Nicholas Murray, editor. **Education in the United States.** 1900.

Butler, Vera M. **Education as Revealed By New England Newspapers prior to 1850.** 1935.

Campbell, Thomas Monroe. **The Movable School Goes to the Negro Farmer.** 1936.

Carter, James G. **Essays upon Popular Education.** 1826.

Carter, James G. **Letters to the Hon. William Prescott, LL.D., on the Free Schools of New England.** 1924.

Channing, William Ellery. **Self-Culture.** 1842.

Coe, George A. **A Social Theory of Religious Education.** 1917.

Committee on Secondary School Studies. **Report of the Committee on Secondary School Studies, Appointed at the Meeting of the National Education Association.** 1893.

Counts, George S. **Dare the School Build a New Social Order?** 1932.

Counts, George S. **The Selective Character of American Secondary Education.** 1922.

Counts, George S. **The Social Composition of Boards of Education.** 1927.

Culver, Raymond B. **Horace Mann and Religion in the Massachusetts Public Schools.** 1929.

Curoe, Philip R. V. **Educational Attitudes and Policies of Organized Labor in the United States.** 1926.

Dabney, Charles William. **Universal Education in the South.** 1936.

Dearborn, Ned Harland. **The Oswego Movement in American Education.** 1925.

De Lima, Agnes. **Our Enemy the Child.** 1926.

Dewey, John. **The Educational Situation.** 1902.

Dexter, Franklin B., editor. **Documentary History of Yale University.** 1916.

Eliot, Charles William. **Educational Reform: Essays and Addresses.** 1898.

Ensign, Forest Chester. **Compulsory School Attendance and Child Labor.** 1921.

Fitzpatrick, Edward Augustus. **The Educational Views and Influence of De Witt Clinton.** 1911.

Fleming, Sanford. **Children & Puritanism.** 1933.

Flexner, Abraham. **The American College: A Criticism.** 1908.

Foerster, Norman. **The Future of the Liberal College.** 1938.

Gilman, Daniel Coit. **University Problems in the United States.** 1898.

Hall, Samuel R. **Lectures on School-Keeping.** 1829.

Hall, Stanley G. **Adolescence: Its Psychology and Its Relations to Physiology, Anthropology, Sociology, Sex, Crime, Religion, and Education.** 1905. 2 vols.

Hansen, Allen Oscar. **Early Educational Leadership in the Ohio Valley.** 1923.

Harris, William T. **Psychologic Foundations of Education.** 1899.

Harris, William T. **Report of the Committee of Fifteen on the Elementary School.** 1895.

Harveson, Mae Elizabeth. **Catharine Esther Beecher: Pioneer Educator.** 1932.

Jackson, George Leroy. **The Development of School Support in Colonial Massachusetts.** 1909.

Kandel, I. L., editor. **Twenty-five Years of American Education.** 1924.

Kemp, William Webb. **The Support of Schools in Colonial New York by the Society for the Propagation of the Gospel in Foreign Parts.** 1913.

Kilpatrick, William Heard. **The Dutch Schools of New Netherland and Colonial New York.** 1912.

Kilpatrick, William Heard. **The Educational Frontier.** 1933.

Knight, Edgar Wallace. **The Influence of Reconstruction on Education in the South.** 1913.

Le Duc, Thomas. **Piety and Intellect at Amherst College, 1865-1912.** 1946.

Maclean, John. **History of the College of New Jersey from Its Origin in 1746 to the Commencement of 1854.** 1877.

Maddox, William Arthur. **The Free School Idea in Virginia before the Civil War.** 1918.

Mann, Horace. **Lectures on Education.** 1855.

McCadden, Joseph J. **Education in Pennsylvania, 1801-1835, and Its Debt to Roberts Vaux.** 1855.

McCallum, James Dow. **Eleazar Wheelock.** 1939.

McCuskey, Dorothy. **Bronson Alcott, Teacher.** 1940.

Meiklejohn, Alexander. **The Liberal College.** 1920.

Miller, Edward Alanson. **The History of Educational Legislation in Ohio from 1803 to 1850.** 1918.

Miller, George Frederick. **The Academy System of the State of New York.** 1922.

Monroe, Will S. **History of the Pestalozzian Movement in the United States.** 1907.

Mosely Education Commission. **Reports of the Mosely Education Commission to the United States of America October-December, 1903.** 1904.

Mowry, William A. **Recollections of a New England Educator.** 1908.

Mulhern, James. **A History of Secondary Education in Pennsylvania.** 1933.

National Herbart Society. **National Herbart Society Yearbooks 1-5, 1895-1899.** 1895-1899.

Nearing, Scott. **The New Education: A Review of Progressive Educational Movements of the Day.** 1915.

Neef, Joseph. **Sketches of a Plan and Method of Education.** 1808.

Nock, Albert Jay. **The Theory of Education in the United States.** 1932.

Norton, A. O., editor. **The First State Normal School in America: The Journals of Cyrus Pierce and Mary Swift.** 1926.

Oviatt, Edwin. **The Beginnings of Yale, 1701-1726.** 1916.

Packard, Frederic Adolphus. **The Daily Public School in the United States.** 1866.

Page, David P. **Theory and Practice of Teaching.** 1848.

Parker, Francis W. **Talks on Pedagogics: An Outline of the Theory of Concentration.** 1894.

Peabody, Elizabeth Palmer. **Record of a School.** 1835.

Porter, Noah. **The American Colleges and the American Public.** 1870.

Reigart, John Franklin. **The Lancasterian System of Instruction in the Schools of New York City.** 1916.

Reilly, Daniel F. **The School Controversy (1891-1893).** 1943.

Rice, Dr. J. M. **The Public-School System of the United States.** 1893.

Rice, Dr. J. M. **Scientific Management in Education.** 1912.

Ross, Early D. **Democracy's College: The Land-Grant Movement in the Formative Stage.** 1942.

Rugg, Harold, et al. **Curriculum-Making: Past and Present.** 1926.

Rugg, Harold, et al. **The Foundations of Curriculum-Making.** 1926.

Rugg, Harold and Shumaker, Ann. **The Child-Centered School.** 1928.

Seybolt, Robert Francis. **Apprenticeship and Apprenticeship Education in Colonial New England and New York.** 1917.

Seybolt, Robert Francis. **The Private Schools of Colonial Boston.** 1935.

Seybolt, Robert Francis. **The Public Schools of Colonial Boston.** 1935.

Sheldon, Henry D. **Student Life and Customs.** 1901.

Sherrill, Lewis Joseph. **Presbyterian Parochial Schools, 1846-1870.** 1932 .

Siljestrom, P. A. **Educational Institutions of the United States.** 1853.

Small, Walter Herbert. **Early New England Schools.** 1914.

Soltes, Mordecai. **The Yiddish Press: An Americanizing Agency.** 1925.

Stewart, George, Jr. **A History of Religious Education in Connecticut to the Middle of the Nineteenth Century.** 1924.

Storr, Richard J. **The Beginnings of Graduate Education in America.** 1953.

Stout, John Elbert. **The Development of High-School Curricula in the North Central States from 1860 to 1918.** 1921.

Suzzallo, Henry. **The Rise of Local School Supervision in Massachusetts.** 1906.

Swett, John. **Public Education in California.** 1911.

Tappan, Henry P. **University Education.** 1851.

Taylor, Howard Cromwell. **The Educational Significance of the Early Federal Land Ordinances.** 1921.

Taylor, J. Orville. **The District School.** 1834.

Tewksbury, Donald G. **The Founding of American Colleges and Universities before the Civil War.** 1932.

Thorndike, Edward L. **Educational Psychology.** 1913-1914.

True, Alfred Charles. **A History of Agricultural Education in the United States, 1785-1925.** 1929.

True, Alfred Charles. **A History of Agricultural Extension Work in the United States, 1785-1923.** 1928.

Updegraff, Harlan. **The Origin of the Moving School in Massachusetts.** 1908.

Wayland, Francis. **Thoughts on the Present Collegiate System in the United States.** 1842.

Weber, Samuel Edwin. **The Charity School Movement in Colonial Pennsylvania.** 1905.

Wells, Guy Fred. **Parish Education in Colonial Virginia.** 1923.

Wickersham, J. P. **The History of Education in Pennsylvania.** 1885.

Woodward, Calvin M. **The Manual Training School.** 1887.

Woody, Thomas. **Early Quaker Education in Pennsylvania.** 1920.

Woody, Thomas. **Quaker Education in the Colony and State of New Jersey.** 1923.

Wroth, Lawrence C. **An American Bookshelf, 1755.** 1934.

Series II

Adams, Evelyn C. **American Indian Education.** 1946.

Bailey, Joseph Cannon. **Seaman A. Knapp: Schoolmaster of American Agriculture.** 1945.

Beecher, Catharine and Harriet Beecher Stowe. **The American Woman's Home.** 1869.

Benezet, Louis T. **General Education in the Progressive College.** 1943.

Boas, Louise Schutz. **Woman's Education Begins.** 1935.

Bobbitt, Franklin. **The Curriculum.** 1918.

Bode, Boyd H. **Progressive Education at the Crossroads.** 1938.

Bourne, William Oland. **History of the Public School Society of the City of New York.** 1870.

Bronson, Walter C. **The History of Brown University, 1764-1914.** 1914.

Burstall, Sara A. **The Education of Girls in the United States.** 1894.

Butts, R. Freeman. **The College Charts Its Course.** 1939.

Caldwell, Otis W. and Stuart A. Courtis. **Then & Now in Education, 1845-1923.** 1923.

Calverton, V. F. & Samuel D. Schmalhausen, editors. **The New Generation: The Intimate Problems of Modern Parents and Children.** 1930.

Charters, W. W. **Curriculum Construction.** 1923.

Childs, John L. **Education and Morals.** 1950.

Childs, John L. **Education and the Philosophy of Experimentalism.** 1931.

Clapp, Elsie Ripley. **Community Schools in Action.** 1939.

Counts, George S. **The American Road to Culture: A Social Interpretation of Education in the United States.** 1930.

Counts, George S. **School and Society in Chicago.** 1928.

Finegan, Thomas E. **Free Schools.** 1921.

Fletcher, Robert Samuel. **A History of Oberlin College.** 1943.

Grattan, C. Hartley. **In Quest of Knowledge: A Historical Perspective on Adult Education.** 1955.

Hartman, Gertrude & Ann Shumaker, editors. **Creative Expression.** 1932.

Kandel, I. L. **The Cult of Uncertainty.** 1943.

Kandel, I. L. **Examinations and Their Substitutes in the United States.** 1936.

Kilpatrick, William Heard. **Education for a Changing Civilization.** 1926.

Kilpatrick, William Heard. **Foundations of Method.** 1925.

Kilpatrick, William Heard. **The Montessori System Examined.** 1914.

Lang, Ossian H., editor. **Educational Creeds of the Nineteenth Century.** 1898.

Learned, William S. **The Quality of the Educational Process in the United States and in Europe.** 1927.

Meiklejohn, Alexander. **The Experimental College.** 1932.

Middlekauff, Robert. **Ancients and Axioms: Secondary Education in Eighteenth-Century New England.** 1963.

Norwood, William Frederick. **Medical Education in the United States Before the Civil War.** 1944.

Parsons, Elsie W. Clews. **Educational Legislation and Administration of the Colonial Governments.** 1899.

Perry, Charles M. **Henry Philip Tappan: Philosopher and University President.** 1933.

Pierce, Bessie Louise. **Civic Attitudes in American School Textbooks.** 1930.

Rice, Edwin Wilbur. **The Sunday-School Movement (1780-1917) and the American Sunday-School Union (1817-1917).** 1917.

Robinson, James Harvey. **The Humanizing of Knowledge.** 1924.

Ryan, W. Carson. **Studies in Early Graduate Education.** 1939.

Seybolt, Robert Francis. **The Evening School in Colonial America.** 1925.

Seybolt, Robert Francis. **Source Studies in American Colonial Education.** 1925.

Todd, Lewis Paul. **Wartime Relations of the Federal Government and the Public Schools, 1917-1918.** 1945.

Vandewalker, Nina C. **The Kindergarten in American Education.** 1908.

Ward, Florence Elizabeth. **The Montessori Method and the American School.** 1913.

West, Andrew Fleming. **Short Papers on American Liberal Education.** 1907.

Wright, Marion M. Thompson. **The Education of Negroes in New Jersey.** 1941.

Supplement

The Social Frontier (Frontiers of Democracy). Vols. 1-10, 1934-1943.